Leasing: Experiences and Expectations

by Patrick J. Davey
Senior Research Associate

A Research Report from The Conference Board

Contents

Tables

Exhibits

About This Report

This report examines the practices and attitudes of corporations that rely, to varying degrees, on leasing to obtain the use of assets. It explains what and why firms lease, and explores the increasingly popular technique of leveraged leasing. In addition, it contains sections on the impact of tax and accounting rules and on the outlook for leasing.

Among its principal findings:

• Few companies reject leasing out of hand. Most view it as a worthwhile financing alternative and employ it whenever an appropriate occasion arises.

• Qualitative as well as quantitative criteria underlie leasing judgments. Though often assigned to financial executives, decision-making responsibility on leases varies and sometimes is fixed by the amount or duration of a lease, or both.

• Leveraged leases have been used primarily in connection with leases involving total payments of more than $1 million for conventional assets, such as railcars and computers, and for esoteric items like satellites. Lessees find such arrangements offer cost and other advantages that make them attractive financing approaches under certain circumstances.

• Most respondents are reasonably content with Standard No. 13 of the Financial Accounting Standards Board, Accounting for Leases, although some recommend changes in it.

• Surveyed lessees differ on the outlook for leasing over the next few years. Forecasts run the gamut from higher to lower usage. And some profess uncertainty, maintaining that circumstances—costs and capital requirements, for example—will determine whether their reliance on leasing increases during the next few years. Lessors and leasing packagers, however, are pretty much agreed that the future direction of leasing points only one way: up.

Profile of Participants

The vast majority of respondents are large companies. While the annual sales of these 118 firms, whose experiences as lessees are represented, extend from just over $30 million to well in excess of $10 billion, only five fall below the $100 million mark.

Seventy-two are in the over $1 billion category. Industrials predominate among surveyed lessees, but they also include utilities, transportation, wholesale-retail, and mining companies (see accompanying tabulation).

Besides responding to questionnaires, some executives provided supplementary information during follow-up meetings. Conversations with officials of leasing companies also elicited details on current leasing activities. So, too, did interviews with both investment and commercial bankers, as well as with other experts who arrange leases. In all, a score of executives provided insights during discussions.

Respondents by Industries	Number of Companies

Manufacturing

Aircraft and aerospace products	3
Blast furnaces, steel mills	3
Chemicals and allied products	14
Construction materials	4
Containers	2
Electronic products	4
Ethical and proprietary drugs	1
Food and kindred products	5
Forest products	3
Machinery and equipment	11
Metal products	2
Miscellaneous consumer products	5
Miscellaneous industrial products	9
Motor vehicles, parts and equipment	5
Office, computing and accounting equipment	3
Petroleum products	10
Rubber and plastic products	4
Total manufacturing	**88**

Nonmanufacturing

Transportation	8
Mining	3
Wholesale and retail trade	7
Utilities	12
Total nonmanufacturing	**30**
Total companies	**118**

Foreword

EFFECTIVELY and efficiently financing the acquisition of capital assets is a recurring issue for management. Commonplace responses such as outright purchases with available funds are neither always possible nor practical. Sometimes leasing offers the best solution.

Despite its attractions as a means of securing the use of assets, leasing is not without its drawbacks. To help potential or actual corporate lessees assess these pros and cons, The Conference Board has on several past occasions examined various aspects of leasing. Most recently, in 1968, it published *Leasing in Industry* (Studies in Business Policy, No. 127), an exhaustive review of company practices that is still useful because it contains information of a timeless character—on negotiation and evaluation approaches, for example. But in the twelve years that have passed since that study was finished, two significant developments have occurred: the evolution of leveraged leasing and the implementation of new accounting rules. To determine their impact and to explore current leasing activity the Board provides an update of its earlier research in this report.

Senior financial executives and other top management officials, including directors, should find this report useful, especially if their companies are actively leasing or seriously considering doing so. Financial analysts, division managers, and others involved in the acquisition of capital assets should also find it helpful. Even individuals from lessor organizations and intermediary firms (such as underwriters) should benefit from the insights it provides into lessees' grievances and expectations.

The Conference Board is obliged to the 118 executives who responded to questionnaires, and especially to those among them who elaborated on their replies during subsequent interviews. It is also indebted to several representatives of the variegated fellowship of lessors and middlemen for information provided during discussions or critiques of the manuscript. This report is a product of the Board's Financial Management Research Department, James K. Brown, Director, which is a unit of the Management Research Division, Harold Stieglitz, Vice President.

KENNETH A. RANDALL
President

Chapter 1
Leasing in Perspective

LEASING was once frowned upon by many as an expensive and, therefore, undesirable financing approach, employed only by companies unable to secure the use of assets by other methods. However, this is seldom the case today. (Only three of the 118 companies contributing their experiences to this survey completely shun leasing.) Now, most view leasing as simply one of several acceptable alternatives to be weighed in connection with the financing of assets.

What caused this change? A number of events following World War II—among them credit crunches; rapid introductions of new and unproven machines, including computers; switches in marketing strategies by manufacturers; and tax changes—helped make leasing more palatable. But perhaps the greatest stimulus of all was that lent by the wide-scale, direct entry of commercial banks into the leasing industry during the 1960's. This development, coupled with aggressive moves by independent lessors—such as assuming high residual values in connection with equipment leases—did much to uplift the status, as well as spur the volume, of leasing.

While precise figures are lacking, it is nevertheless clear that industrial leasing constitutes a big business. Available estimates suggest that the original value of all outstanding equipment leases in 1979 amounted to $150 billion, and that leasing currently finances some 20 percent of all capital equipment acquisitions.[1]

[1] Oil and gas leases, which detail the operating obligations and contingent rights of contracting parties, are not reviewed in this report.

The Leasing Market

The leasing market enables companies with asset needs to get together with others capable of filling them. But the same can be said of other asset-based markets—those centered on conditional sales agreements, or chattel mortgages, for example. What distinguishes the leasing market is not the parties involved, but rather the legal and tax implications that are attached to leasing.

Lessees do not own the assets they use; lessors do. Lessees are permitted to claim rental payments on the assets they lease as tax deductions. In contrast, purchasers of assets employing techniques such as conditional sales agreements to acquire the assets are regarded as owners from the outset for tax purposes, even though full title is not transmitted to them until all the contract terms are fulfilled. The reasons and ways in which parties to leases are responsive to their tax implications are treated in Chapter 3.

Participants

There are always at least two participants in a leasing transaction—a lessee and a lessor. Frequently the total is greater, numbering five or even more. The supporting players may include packagers, debt participants, attorneys and other furnishers of services.

Lessees include virtually all kinds of companies, from the very small to the very large. They comprise financially strong as well as marginal firms, although a recently completed

Leasing Terminology

Except where the context suggests otherwise, the words "lease" and "leasing" as used here generally pertain to the activities of lessees in obtaining the use of assets. Definitions of other terms appearing in this report that may be unfamiliar to some readers follow:

• *Bargain Purchase Option*—a right granted a lessee to buy a leased asset at a price below its expected fair market value when exercisable.
• *Contingent Rentals*—portions of stipulated lease payments that are conditional or that depend on variables such as the prime interest rate.
• *Executory Costs*—outlays sometimes included in lease payments to cover such expenses as those for insurance and maintenance.
• *Implicit Interest Rate*—the effective rate of interest paid by lessees to finance through leases.
• *Incremental Borrowing Rate*—the interest rate a lessee would have to pay to borrow the sum required to buy a leased asset.
• *Master Lease*—an open-end agreement that permits a lessee to obtain both the use of currently needed assets and, at its discretion, and without negotiating a completely new contract, assets for which needs arise in the future.
• *Residual Value*—the fair market value of a leased asset at the expiration of the lease term. Guarantees are sometimes used to limit the risks inherent in the assumption of residual values by lessors.
• *Leveraged Leasing*—a special leasing arrangement in which borrowed funds constitute a portion of a lessor's investment in a leased asset.
• *Sensitivity Analysis*—a computer-facilitated statistical technique that enables lessees to determine the relative importance of assumptions, such as those on residual values, which are critical to decision making.
• *Trustee*—an entity, often a commercial bank or trust company that, for a fee, acts on behalf of parties it represents. In leveraged lease transactions, owners' trustees may protect the interest of equity participants and indenture trustees, those of debt participants.

study finds that weaker organizations tend to rely more heavily on leasing.[2] Basically all companies with continuing capital equipment needs are actual or potential lessees. And those among them in cyclical industries, such as air transportation, are more likely to appear as lessees.

Lessors fall into four main groups: individuals, usually wealthy and sometimes operating as partners; independent leasing companies; bank-related organizations; and captive leasing companies. Others that occasionally appear as lessors include pension trusts, insurance companies, educational and religious institutions, and industrial development agencies. Exactly how many lessors exist is uncertain, but as a general indication it is known that a recent survey of the American Association of Equipment Lessors was directed to its 600 members.[3]

Individuals in high tax brackets can be competitive as lessors, but because of limitations on their use of the investment tax credit—and because only relatively few deals come to their attention—they are not ordinarily major factors in the market. Commercial banks and to a lesser extent, investment banking firms, are important lessors, as are independent leasing companies. Many captive leasing companies—some of which were organized exclusively to help market their parents' products—have expanded their interests and now provide leasing and other types of financing for nonaffiliated firms. In the process they have become important factors in the leasing market. Like individual lessors, the corporate variety often act in consort, especially when the amounts involved are substantial or when the desire to limit risk prompts diversification.

Supporting Players

Brokers, or, as they are also called, packagers, syndicators or underwriters often assume important roles in counseling on and ef-

[2]William L. Ferrara, James B. Thies, and Mark W. Dirsmith, *The Lease-Purchase Decision.* New York. National Association of Accountants, 1980.

[3]American Association of Equipment Lessors, *1979 Survey of Accounting and Business Practices.* Arlington, Virginia.

fectuating leases. For a fee, these organizations arrange leasing deals between prospective lessors and lessees. On occasion they even appear as principals in arrangements by making a small equity investment as an inducement to attract other potential investors. Investment and commercial banks sometimes assume the mantle of a broker but in that capacity they usually shun direct investment in the leased asset to prevent any hint of impropriety. Because of the special niche packagers fill in connection with the accomplishment of leveraged leases, their activities are more fully detailed in Chapter 3.

Debt investors, usually insurance companies, commercial banks, or pension funds, commonly have a stake in leveraged leases (see below, pages 20-22). Appealing rates and relatively secure exposures make such participation attractive for these organizations.

Attorneys prepare the documentation for lease agreements, and also issue opinions on a variety of lease-related matters. In nonstandard cases, these can prove to be time-consuming and expensive chores.

Trustees, representing equity and debt participants, respectively, are sometimes used in connection with lease transactions. They facilitate administration when several lessors or lenders are involved in a lease transaction. In addition, companies such as insurance firms sometimes employ trustees to act as lessors for them to avoid legal constraints on their activities. The responsibilities of trustees, primarily to service the interests they represent, are spelled out in trust agreements.

Kinds of Leases

Leasing is a financing method that enables one organization to secure the use of an asset from another that owns it in return for certain considerations—notably rental fees. Individual arrangements between lessors and lessees are detailed in two basic types of leases: financial and operating.

Financial or finance leases are long-term arrangements whose duration tends to match the useful life of the asset. Lessors usually recoup their initial investment, various other costs, and a profit from these leases. Such leases tend to be noncancelable.

Operating leases run for a period considerably less than the asset's useful life. These leases can normally be canceled by lessees, and so are often employed to obtain the use of assets needed for relatively brief periods or subject to possible rapid obsolescence—computers, for instance. Lessors seldom, if ever, recover their total costs during the initial term of an operating lease. Therefore, to come out ahead, they must arrange subsequent leases or profitably dispose of the asset at the conclusion of the original lease term.

There are hybrids and variations of these basic lease forms. Principal among them are sale and leasebacks, leveraged leases, and full-service leases. In a sale and leaseback, the owner of an asset—an expensive machine, for instance—sells it to a second party and simultaneously agrees to lease it back from the purchaser. This enables the company to augment its working capital without impairing its operating ability.

Leveraged leasing, discussed in detail in Chapter 3, introduces a third party, a debt purveyor, into the leasing transaction, with advantages to lessors and lessees. Service or maintenance leases impose upkeep or administrative responsiblities—repairing or record keeping, typically—as well as financing ones on lessors, though not without cost to lessees.

Current Uses of Leasing

Virtually anything can be leased, but everything cannot be leased economically. For the most part, companies tend to lease assets of a supportive character—vehicles and computers, primarily—and to purchase assets of a productive nature—machinery, for example. Table 1 details applications of leasing among study respondents.

Reasons for Leasing

Queried lessees offer five major reasons for engaging in leasing transactions: economy, flex-

Table 1: Applications of Leasing among Respondents[1]

Asset Leased	Number of Mentions
Transportation equipment	91
Computers and office equipment	77
Buildings and space	68
Production equipment	13
Fuel and fuel-supply equipment	8
Other	6

[1]For a longer laundry list, see Appendix, page 42.

ibility, convenience, risk avoidance, and necessity. The emphasis often varies, depending upon the kind of asset that is being leased. Working capital conservation or improvement and off-balance sheet financing are seldom mentioned as incentives for leasing.

Some lessees turn to leasing because unprofitable operations or other circumstances make it impossible to enjoy the depreciation and investment-credit tax advantages (subsequently discussed) that attach to ownership. They find that lessors are willing to flow through at least a portion of these benefits in the form of lower rates. And a number maintain that leasing can be economical when lessors share the cash-flow advantages they reap—through economies of scale or realization of higher residual values—with them by making rates attractive compared with those for borrowing.

A number of utilities arrange nuclear fuel leases or "heat supply contracts." They find these arrangements provide cash-flow advantages as well as lower financing costs.

Other lessees hold that leasing gives greater flexibility than ownership; it fills their needs, particularly in situations where these are temporary or where the period of utility of the asset is expected to be less than its useful life. If, for example, a trailer is needed for three years, a lease for that exact term can usually be arranged, but not a purchase. One utility entered into a turbine lease because, though expensive, it furnished needed generating capacity not otherwise immediately available.

Still others, anxious to avoid problems such as those that attach to the administration and maintenance of automotive fleets, opt for leasing because it offers them the desired relief. Besides the convenience of service, such leases also enable them to avoid disposal problems.

Companies that lease electronic data- processing equipment and other office equipment (including duplication machines) only infrequently cite savings as a motivator. Often their main impetus for leasing is to steer clear of possible obsolescence in an area where technological advancement has been rapid. In effect, leasing protects them from the risks of ownership, albeit at a price that reflects such insurance.

Sites lessees of warehouses, stores, office space, terminals and production facilities, claim they often have no choice but to lease. Locations in shopping malls, for example, may only be obtained through rentals.

The rationale for leasing expressed in the following comments by participants is typical:

"As we are not, at this time, in a position to utilize the benefits associated with the investment tax credit (ITC) but are, however, involved in an extremely capital-intensive industry, virtually all high unit value (over $50,000) equipment items are considered to be candidates for leasing financing. We take this approach because, through the use of leasing, the lessor is able to pass to us, in the form of a lower interest cost, the tax benefits associated with ITC and accelerated depreciation."

Vice president and treasurer,
a transportation company

*　　*　　*　　*

"We. . . lease some assets, such as transportation equipment, computers, branch warehouses, office space, and standard office equipment for the following reasons:

"To maintain the flexibility necessary to take advantage of the newest innovations in areas of fast technological change (selected computers and office equipment).

"To maintain the flexibility to change quickly branch and office size or location when the market changes.

"To take advantage of maintenance provisions of leases where maintenance is deemed important (selected office equipment).

"To obtain procurement and management services on salesmen's leased cars scattered throughout the United States and Canada.

"To secure facilities in a desired location when purchase is not possible or practical (real estate).

"To fulfill a temporary need (less than 12 months)."

Vice president and controller,
a metal products company

*　　*　　*　　*

"When we do lease, it is because we perceive the lease alternative to be less costly than the purchase alternative. Usually this occurs when (1) our venture partners are not generating sufficient taxable income to benefit from investment tax credits in a timely manner, or (2) we perceive that the likely residual value of the leased equipment at the end of the lease term will be significantly lower than the residual value assumed by the lessor."

Director of finance,
a mining company

Reasons for Not Leasing

Cost considerations underlie the postures of the three surveyed concerns that completely shun leasing. These firms simply find ownership of assets more economical. Only cash-flow problems or changes in tax regulations would prompt them to alter their stance.

Of course, other participants limit the amount of leasing they do for similar reasons. Some balk because they hesitate to surrender residual values in the prevailing inflationary climate. And a couple of utilities curtail their leasing activities because, in the words of one: "Lease property does not become a part of the rate base on which we can earn a rate of return."

Chapter 2
Corporations as Lessees

WHEN to consider leasing and how to go about it are questions that most users of capital assets have resolved. What follows traces the paths participants have chosen and also explores the problems they have experienced along the way.

Policies and Guidelines

Written policies on leasing are in the minority among respondents. Just over 10 percent (14) have them, although several others indicate such statements are currently in the process of preparation. Some of these directives consist solely of succinct declarations of philosophy. An example is that of a forest products company: "Equipment may be leased only if it is to the overall financial benefit of the company or if there are . . . overriding operational considerations which favor leasing." But more frequently they are fairly detailed pronouncements that include procedural instructions and other information as well (see Exhibit 1).

The vast majority of surveyed companies prefer to employ general guidelines, often issued in bulletins, to direct their leasing activities. But whether formal or informal, such outlines reflect one of three attitudes toward leasing. In order of frequency of mention they are:

• A bias against it—leasing should be used, for instance, only when no other alternative is available.

• Neutrality—economics should be the paramount criterion in deciding whether or not to lease.

• Encouragement—leasing should be used to take advantage of existing conditions, such as inability to absorb the tax benefits that attach to capital outlays.

Whatever their form, written guidelines typically have two elements in common besides the articulation and perhaps explanation of the sponsoring concern's stance on leasing: (1) definitions of essential items, and (2) procedures to follow in connection with the analysis, review and authorization of arrangements. Preprinted forms calling for data to facilitate the approval process may be appended (see Exhibit 2).

Evaluation Approaches

Where operational influences—services or protection from obsolescence, for example—are not paramount, leasing decisions are usually based on economic considerations. In most companies the decision to invest in the asset has already been made and the leasing decision is merely a choice among financing alternatives.

Here are some capsule descriptions of how participating companies go about the evaluation of leasing proposals:

"An in-house computer program has been developed to help determine the cost of funds

Exhibit 1: Leasing Policy Statement—Northrop Corporation

Subject: LEASING PROGRAM

Date: 29 June 1979

I. POLICY

  A. It is the policy of the company to purchase capital assets and to finance such purchases from internally generated funds, bank loans, or other corporate financing. Exceptions to this policy, which may justify leasing, are listed below:

    1. The property is required for a period substantially shorter than its normally expected life, and the lease is less costly than purchase of the property.

    2. The property has a high obsolescence factor, and the lessor assumes financial risk of obsolescence, residual value, and disposal so that the ultimate cost to Northrop is less than the cost of ownership, or the amount payable to the lessor for assuming such risks is not unreasonable.

    3. The need is immediate, lease property is available at a reasonable price, and purchasable property is either unavailable or is not available within the time requirements.

    4. Lease property is advantageously located and purchasable property is not available with similar location advantages.

    5. The lessor can purchase property and/or provide service at less cost than Northrop could so that the overall cost of leasing is less than Northrop ownership cost.

    6. There is a requirement for foreign real property, company ownership of such property is impractical or impossible, and the cost will be charged directly to a contract.

The U.S. Government's policy of disallowing the difference in cost between leasing over a given period and purchasing should be taken into account when a lease is being considered.

  B. Operating leases (see Section III.F. for definition) not exceeding $100,000 gross lease payments per year are to be processed entirely within the lessee company element. Operating leases that exceed $100,000 require the prior approval of the Corporate Vice President-Administration and Services. On programs where it is necessary to enter into operating leases involving foreign real property for which costs will be charged directly to the contract, the cognizant materiel manager may submit a written request to the Corporate Vice President-Administration and Services for advance approval to obtain such leases without submitting each one to the Corporate Office. A copy of each fully executed real property lease, regardless of dollar amount, is to be provided to the Corporate Vice President-Administration and Services.

  C. When rented property is used in common by various company elements, the advantages and possibilities of arranging for a master lease are to be explored by the Corporate Vice President-Administration and Services and by the cognizant personnel of the affected company elements.

II. RESPONSIBILITY

  Company elements shall advise the Corporate Vice President-Administration and Services whenever communications with real estate brokers, property owners, or community industrial development organizations take place, and whenever visits are made to real property being considered for leasing purposes. The Corporate Vice President-Administration and Services shall ensure that such communications and visits are in consonance with the corporatewide facilities management program.

Exhibit 1: Leasing Policy Statement—Northrop Corporation (continued)

A. Capital Lease Proposals:

1. Company elements shall submit proposed capital leases for real or personal property to the Corporate Vice President-Administration and Services for Corporate Office review and approval. In preparing such proposals, company elements shall:

a. Review CFM 8-403, "Lease Versus Purchase-Financing Cost Comparison" prior to submitting lease proposals for Corporate Office approval.
b. To the fullest extent possible, include the following information in the lease proposal:

1) A description of the property to be leased, including its location, and the term of the lease.
2) A justification of the decision to lease, including an evaluation of lease versus purchase costs and the effects on insurance, taxes, interest on capital invested, maintenance, other overhead costs, and the salvage value, if applicable, in accordance with CFM No. 8-403.
3) The method and place of financing.
4) The lessor's financial responsibility and obligation in connection with the lease.

2. The Corporate Vice President-Administration and Services shall review and, if appropriate, grant preliminary approval to proposed capital leases. The review shall consist of coordination with:

a. The Corporate Director-Banking Administration for analysis of the financing costs involved and comparison with the currently prevailing incremental costs of borrowing.
b. The Senior Vice President and General Counsel for analysis of the proposed terms and conditions.

Capital lease proposals approved by the Corporate Vice President-Administration and Services shall be forwarded to the Corporate Director-Banking Administration.

3. The Corporate Director-Banking Administration shall review all capital lease proposals approved by the Corporate Vice President-Administration and Services, and shall have final approval authority for those with alternative purchase cost up to $500,000. Those with alternative purchase cost in excess of $500,000 shall be forwarded to the Senior Vice President-Finance for final approval.

4. In exceptional cases where immediate action is desirable, approval may be obtained by telephone from the Corporate Vice President-Administration and Services. Such an approval must be followed by the normally required review and written approvals.

B. Capital Lease Commitments:

1. The cognizant legal counsel shall be responsible for preparation and/or review of definitive lease commitments and, through the Corporate Vice President-Administration and Services, shall coordinate such commitments with the Corporate Director-Tax Administration and the Corporate Director-Risk Management.
2. In general, all leases shall be signed by the authorized official of the lessee company element. The Corporate Vice President-Administration and Services shall ordinarily sign Corporate Office

leases, although other signatories authorized by the Northrop Board of Directors may also execute such documents. Leases for data processing equipment which exceed $100,000 total gross lease payments over the term of the lease shall be reviewed and signed by the Corporate Vice President-Administration and Services.

    3. Company elements shall provide a copy of each fully executed capital lease to the Corporate Vice President-Administration and Services, who shall retain such copy in a corporate lease file after routing it to the Corporate Vice President-Controller for information purposes.

C. Company elements shall provide a copy of each fully executed real property lease to the Corporate Vice President-Administration and Services.

III. DEFINITIONS

For the purposes of this directive, the following definitions shall apply:

A. A *lease* shall mean a contract agreement or purchase order relating to the use of real or personal property for a period of time at a specified rent.
B. *Real property* shall mean land or building or land and buildings.
C. *Personal property* shall mean all property except real property, e.g., machinery and equipment not permanently attached to real property.
D. *"Rental payment"* and *"lease payment"* shall be synonymous.
E. A *renewal* is an extension of the lease period. The original period of use and all renewals are cumulative in determining whether a lease is to be specified as a capital lease or as an operating lease.
F. A lease is defined as a *capital lease* if it meets any one of the following criteria:

    1. The lease transfers ownership of the property to the lessee by the end of the lease term, or
    2. The lease contains a bargain purchase option, or
    3. The lease term is equal to at least 75 percent of the estimated economic life of the leased property. This criteria does not apply if the beginning of the term falls within the last 25 percent of the total estimated life, or
    4. The present value of the minimum lease payments at the beginning of the lease term equals 90 percent of the fair value of the leased property, less any related investment tax credit retained by the lessor. The minimum payments for the purpose of this test exclude that portion of the payments representing executory costs such as insurance, maintenance, and taxes paid to the lessor, including any profit thereon.
G. A lease is defined as an *operating lease* if it does not meet the criteria of III.F. Operating leases shall not be capitalized.

Chairman and
Chief Executive Officer

Exhibit 2: Authority for Lease Form—A Machinery Manufacturing Company

Authority For Lease

UNIT		BUDGET YEAR	BUDGET CAT. & ITEM	AFL NO.	
				CAPITAL ☐	
				OPERATING ☐	
LESSOR'S NAME			RELATED DOCUMENTS	ANNUAL AMOUNT	

LEASE REGISTER

LEASE START DATE	INTENDED END DATE	MINIMUM LEASE TERM	EST. ECONOMIC LIFE	% OF TERM TO ECON. LIFE
INVEST. TAX CREDIT ☐ RETAINED BY LESSOR	DOES TITLE PASS TO DEERE?	BARGAIN PURCHASE	FAIR VALUE	% OF TOTAL PRESENT VALUE TO FAIR VALUE
$ ☐ FLOW THRU TO DEERE				

PAYMENTS DUE: ☐ MONTHLY ☐ BI-MONTHLY ☐ QUARTERLY ☐ SEMI-ANNUAL ☐ ANNUAL ☐ OTHER:

	NO. OF PERIODS	AMOUNT PER PERIOD	ANNUAL AMOUNT	TOTAL FOR LEASE TERM	PRESENT VALUE @ _____ %
LEASE PAYMENT AT INTENDED USE LEVEL					
TAX ON LEASE PAYMENT					
TOTAL					
MINIMUM LEASE PAYMENT - EXCL TAX					
DEDUCT EXECUTORY COSTS IN MINIMUM					
SUB TOTAL					
ADD GUARANTEED RESIDUAL VALUE OR BARGAIN PURCHASE AMOUNT					
TOTAL					

DESCRIPTION OF FACILITIES	ACCT. NO.	ANNUAL LEASE AMOUNT	INITIAL EXPENSE

REASONS FOR EXPENDITURE:

FACILITIES TO BE SCRAPPED, SOLD, ABANDONED, OR DEMOLISHED AS RESULT OF THIS AFL.	AFD NO.

REVIEW AND APPROVALS

	DATE		DATE
	DATE		DATE
		UNIT CONTROLLER	
	DATE		DATE
		UNIT MANAGER	
	DATE		DATE
FINANCIAL ANALYSIS DEPT.		DIRECTOR OF MFG. OR DIRECTOR OF MARKETING	
	DATE		DATE
COMPUTER SYSTEMS DEPT.		VICE PRESIDENT	
	DATE		DATE
ENGINEERING DEPT.		SENIOR OFFICER	
	DATE		DATE
SAFETY & ENVIR. DEPT.		BOARD OF DIRECTORS OR EXEC. COMMITTEE	

implied in a lease proposal. The approach is an internal rate of return calculation for the flows of rental payments, depreciation foregone, lost residual, ITC passed to lessor, and capital conserved. The implicit rate derived from the program is then compared with the costs of alternate sources of funds (e.g., bank borrowings, general corporate funds).

"If a lease proposal is competitive or more favorable, based upon the strictly economic evaluations, then noneconomic variables are examined. Examples would include operating considerations, like maintenance, or general management aspects, like balance-sheet treatment or the ability to isolate risk. The sequence in which economic and noneconomic variables are considered can be reversed in some projects."

Project finance specialist,
a petroleum company

* * * *

"Lease proposals are evaluated by comparing the after-tax cash flow associated with owning to the cash flow from leasing and determining the effective interest rate implicit in the lease proposal. The effective interest rate is then compared to either the company's long-term borrowing rate or cost of capital, depending on the nature of the lease. Collateral considerations (e.g., risk of obsolescence, period of time facility will be required, ability to recover residual value, flexibility of operations, etc.) are also taken into account when making the decision."

Director-treasury division,
a chemical company

* * * *

"Major lease proposals are evaluated from both a technical suitability (business risk) and financial (lease vs. buy) viewpoint."

Vice president and treasurer,
a utility company

Financial Analysis

The fundamental problem, of course, is to weigh the costs of leasing against those of owning. To accomplish this task, most undertake discounted cash-flow studies—the sort common in capital expenditure analysis.[1] Two of the most popular methods—one relying on net present value, the other, on internal rate of return—are illustrated in Exhibits 3 and 4. Discounted cash-flow examinations enable companies to overcome two important difficulties in making true comparisons of the costs of ownership with those of leasing: differences in the timing of outlays and inflows, and in the effects of tax regulations.

Not all follow this approach, however. A few participants find them too difficult to apply, or consider leasing a practical, though expensive, means of securing supplementary funds and resort to it only when other financing approaches have been exhausted.

Responsibility for Leasing Decisions

Among surveyed companies, responsibility for leasing decisions is most often entrusted to the vice president-finance or treasurer. However, as Table 2 shows, this responsibility can fall to others—some in areas other than finance.

In seven surveyed firms, decision making on leases is a shared responsibility of two or more individuals or groups. Three of these, for instance, require the joint assent of the corporate treasurer and local managers for lease commitments.

In 23 other companies, authority is divided; where decision-making responsibility resides depends on the amount, duration or type of lease. In one such organization, for example, the treasurer must approve all leases with annual payments of $3,000 or more and basic term of three years or more, while the appropriations

[1]For a detailed review of the principal variations, together with illustrations, see Henry G. Hamel, *Leasing in Industry*, National Industrial Conference Board, Studies on Business Policy, No. 127, 1968. Loan copies of the publication are available from the Board's Information Service.

Exhibit 3: Procedure for Evaluating the Cost of Financial Lease Versus Buy Alternatives—Whirlpool Corporation

When evaluating financial lease versus buy alternatives, it is important to remember that the decision to acquire the asset is likely to have been made already. The financial evaluation revolves around determining the most economical method of financing the acquisition among the alternatives being considered.

The steps to follow in the evaluation are:

1. Determine the present value of the after-tax lease payments.
2. Determine the sum of:
   a. The present value of the cost after tax of purchasing the asset.
   b. The present value of the "debt equivalent" of the lease.
3. Compare the present values calculated in (1) and (2) above to determine the more economical alternative.
4. Consider other relevant factors unique to the operational aspects, lease provisisions, etc.

EXAMPLE OF EVALUATION OF A LEASE VERSUS BUY ALTERNATIVE

The following example will serve to illustrate the method of evaluation.

The company has decided that it requires additional warehousing space. A location has been chosen and the size and type of construction for the building has been determined. The company has contacted several possible lessors, and through a process of elimination, has chosen the one that offers the best leasing proposition, all things considered. An analysis is now to be made to determine whether it is more economical for the company to enter into the lease agreement or buy the warehouse. The following facts are known or assumed:

1. Concerning the lease:
   a. The term of the lease is 20 years
   b. Lease payments are $302,000 annually
2. The warehouse will cost $2,220,000 ($600,000 for the land and $1,620,000 for the building).
3. The company can finance the warehouse through short-term borrowings at the prime rate, which is approximately 6 percent. The company might also finance the project with long-term borrowings at approximately the same rate. (You should contact the Financial Planning & Analysis Department to obtain the actual interest rate to use at any given time.)
4. The company's combined federal and state income tax rates are 50 percent.
5. The company's opportunity cost rate is 10 percent (net of taxes). In other words, the company has other opportunities for investment other than this warehouse which would return an average of 10 percent after tax. (You should contact the Financial Planning & Analysis Department to obtain the actual opportunity cost rate to use at any given time.)
6. The estimated life of the property for depreciation purposes is 40 years.

Illustration 1 shows a comparison of the cost of leasing the warehouse to buying it and borrowing the funds to finance it. It will be noted that this analysis ignores the fact that at the end of the 20-year period, the company would own an asset with a book value of approximately $1,300,000 if it chooses the buy-and-borrow alternative. This, of course, is an additional factor favoring that alternative. It also ignores the possibility of having an option to buy the warehouse from the lessor at the end of the lease period. A method for factoring these two considerations into the analysis will be discussed later.

Going through Illustration 1 item by item:

Line 1 is the present value of a dollar discounted at the rate of 10 percent (the company's opportunity cost) obtained from a standard interest table.

Exhibit 3: Procedure for Evaluating the Cost of Financial Lease   Versus Buy Alternatives—Whirlpool Corporation (continued)

Line 2 is the sum of the annual after-tax lease payments.

Line 3 is the sum of the discounted cash outflows under the proposed lease. This represents the present value of the lease alternative, $1,284,000.

Line 4 represents the present value of the cash outflow required to purchase the land and construct the building, $2,220,000.

Line 5 is the present value of the cash inflows that result from being able to take a deduction for depreciation in the income tax returns during the first twenty years of asset life.

Line 6 is the present value of the cash flows that would result if the company borrowed the money to finance the acquisition. This calls for some explanation. You note that the cash inflow in year zero from the "debt equivalent" exceeds the cost of the asset being acquired. This results from the following:

Under the terms of the lease, the company is required to commit itself to make a stream of payments of $302,000 a year for the next twenty years. The debt equivalent of this commitment is the amount of money the company would receive as the proceeds of a loan if it were willing to obligate itself to make the same stream of payments to amortize the loan. If any other amount were used as the debt equivalent, such as the cost of the asset being acquired, the company could not make a valid comparison of the lease alternative to the buy-and-borrow alternative since it would not be assuming the same obligations under each.

Referring to Illustration 2, the debt equivalent is calculated as follows:

Line 1 is the sum of the annual lease payments.

Line 2 is the present value of a dollar discounted at the rate of 6 percent (the company's assumed borrowing rate) obtained from a standard interest table.

Line 3 is the present value of the lease payments discounted at the rate of 6 percent. This also would be the proceeds of a loan made at 6 percent interest to be amortized over twenty years with annual payments of $302,000.

Lines 4 through 8 merely break the annual payments down into their principal and interest components. We need to know the amount of interest paid annually, because it is allowable as a deduction in the tax returns, from which comes a stream of cash inflows.

Lines 9 through 12 summarize the debt equivalent. Line 9 is the proceeds of the loan. Line 10 is the sum of the cash outflows for the annual payments. Line 11 is the sum of the cash inflows resulting from deducting the interest payments in the income tax returns. Line 12 is the total of all the cash flows making up the debt equivalent which is carried to Illustration 1, line 6.

Returning to Illustration 1:

Line 7 is the sum of the cash flows involved in the buy-and-borrow alternative.

Line 8 is the present value of the cash flows in the buy-and-borrow alternative, discounted at the rate of 10 percent.

It can be seen from Illustration 1 that the buy-and-borrow alternative is more economical than the leasing alternative in this example based upon the prevailing assumptions. The discounted cash outflows for buy and borrow are $453,000, compared to $1,284,000 for leasing.

If the lease agreement includes an option to buy the warehouse at the end of the lease period, we can factor that in by showing a cash outflow in year 21 equal to the purchase price and discounting it to its present value at the company's opportunity cost rate.

If there is no option to purchase the warehouse at the end of the lease period, the fact that the company owns the warehouse under the purchase alternative should be factored in. In order to have an equivalent situation under the lease, the company would have to purchase the warehouse at the end of the lease period for a price at least equal to its book value. Therefore, in the analysis we could show a cash outflow in year 21 of $1,300,000 (book value of the asset) and discount it to its present value (at 10%), adding $176,000 to the cost of the lease alternative, making the buy-and-borrow alternative that much more attractive.

Exhibit 3: Procedure for Evaluating the Cost of Financial Lease Versus Buy Alternatives—Whirlpool Corporation (continued)

Illustration 1

COMPARISON OF LEASE WITH BUY-AND-BORROW
(In Thousands of Dollars)

ANNUAL CASH FLOW TO END OF PERIOD

ITEM	TOTAL	YEAR 0	1	2	3	4	5	6	7	8	9	10	11	12	13	14	15	16	17	18	19	20
Memo:																						
1. Present value of $1 at 10%		1.0000	.9091	.8264	.7513	.6830	.6209	.5645	.5132	.4665	.4241	.3855	.3505	.3186	.2897	.2633	.2394	.2176	.1978	.1799	.1635	.1486
Lease:																						
2. Payments after tax (50% x $302,000 per year before tax) $3,020	$3,020	-	(151)	(151)	(151)	(151)	(151)	(151)	(151)	(151)	(151)	(151)	(151)	(151)	(151)	(151)	(151)	(151)	(151)	(151)	(151)	(151)
3. Discounted cash flow (line 1 x line 2)	($1,284)	-	(137)	(125)	(113)	(103)	(94)	(85)	(77)	(70)	(64)	(58)	(53)	(48)	(44)	(40)	(36)	(33)	(30)	(27)	(25)	(22)
Buy and Borrow:																						
4. Capital Outlay	($2,220)	(2,220)	-	-	-	-	-	-	-	-	-	-	-	-	-	-	-	-	-	-	-	-
5. Depreciation¹ Tax Shield	$ 442	-	30	29	28	27	26	25	24	23	22	22	21	20	19	18	18	18	18	18	18	18
6. Borrow "Debt Equivalent" (Ex. II, line 12)	($1,288)	3,464	(198)	(201)	(204)	(207)	(210)	(214)	(218)	(222)	(226)	(231)	(235)	(241)	(246)	(251)	(257)	(254)	(271)	(278)	(285)	(293)
7. Undiscounted Cash Flow	($3,066)	1,244	(168)	(172)	(176)	(180)	(184)	(189)	(194)	(199)	(204)	(209)	(214)	(221)	(227)	(233)	(239)	(246)	(253)	(260)	(267)	(275)
8. Discounted Cash Flow (line 1 x 7)	($ 453)	1,244	(153)	(142)	(132)	(123)	(114)	(107)	(100)	(93)	(87)	(81)	(75)	(70)	(66)	(61)	(57)	(54)	(50)	(47)	(44)	(41)

Note 1: Depreciation figured at 150° declining balance until the point is reached when straight line depreciation exceeds declining balance, then switch to straight line method. Combined income tax rate is 50%.

Exhibit 3: Procedure for Evaluating the Cost of Financial Lease Versus Buy Alternatives—Whirlpool Corporation (continued)

Illustration 2

THE DEBT EQUIVALENT OF THE LEASE
(In Thousands of Dollars)

ANNUAL CASH FLOW TO END OF PERIOD

ITEM	TOTAL	YEAR 0	1	2	3	4	5	6	7	8	9	10	11	12	13	14	15	16	17	18	19	20
Capitalization:																						
1. Lease Payments	($6,040)	-	(302)	(302)	(302)	(302)	(302)	(302)	(302)	(302)	(302)	(302)	(302)	(302)	(302)	(302)	(302)	(302)	(302)	(302)	(302)	(302)
2. Present Value of $1 at 6%	-	1.0000	.9433	.8899	.8396	.7920	.7472	.7049	.6650	.6274	.5918	.5583	.5267	.4969	.4688	.4423	.4172	.3936	.3713	.3503	.3305	.3118
3. Discounted Cash Flow	($3,464)	-	(285)	(269)	(253)	(239)	(226)	(213)	(201)	(189)	(179)	(169)	(159)	(150)	(141)	(134)	(126)	(119)	(112)	(106)	(100)	(94)
Amortization:																						
4. Opening Unpaid Balance			3,464	3,370	3,270	3,164	3,052	2,933	2,807	2,673	2,531	2,381	2,222	2,053	1,874	1,684	1,483	1,270	1,044	805	551	282
5. Payments (line 1)	($6,040)	-	(302)	(302)	(302)	(302)	(302)	(302)	(302)	(302)	(302)	(302)	(302)	(302)	(302)	(302)	(302)	(302)	(302)	(302)	(302)	(302)
6. Interest (6% x line 4)	($2,576)		(208)	(202)	(196)	(190)	(183)	(176)	(168)	(160)	(152)	(143)	(133)	(123)	(112)	(101)	(89)	(76)	(63)	(48)	(33)	(20)[1]
7. Principal (line 5 - 6)	($3,464)		(94)	(100)	(106)	(112)	(119)	(126)	(134)	(142)	(150)	(159)	(169)	(179)	(190)	(201)	(213)	(226)	(239)	(254)	(269)	(282)
8. Closing Unpaid Balance (line 4 - line 7)			3,370	3,270	3,164	3,052	2,933	2,807	2,673	2,531	2,381	2,222	2,053	1,874	1,684	1,483	1,270	1,044	805	551	282	-
Debt Equivalent:																						
9. Cash Proceeds (Total line 3)	$3,464	$3,464																				
10. Payments (line 1)	($6,040)	-	(302)	(302)	(302)	(302)	(302)	(302)	(302)	(302)	(302)	(302)	(302)	(302)	(302)	(302)	(302)	(302)	(302)	(302)	(302)	(302)
11. Tax Reduction on Int. Equivalent (50% of line 6)	$1,288		104	101	98	95	92	88	84	80	76	71	67	61	56	51	49	38	31	24	17	9
12. Net Cash Flow After Tax	($1,288)	$3,464	($198)	($201)	($204)	($207)	($210)	($214)	($218)	($222)	($226)	($231)	($235)	($241)	($246)	($251)	($257)	($264)	($271)	($278)	($285)	($293)

Note 1: Difference due to rounding.

Exhibit 4: Methodology for Lease Versus Buy Analysis—A Diversified Manufacturing Company

A. Definitions

The lease versus buy decision is a *financing* decision, not an *investment* decision. This means that when doing a lease versus buy analysis, the decision to obtain use of an asset is assumed to have been made; the lease-and-buy alternatives are merely two options for obtaining use of the asset. This distinction is made here since it largely determines the methodology for a lease-versus-buy analysis. Namely, as a method of financing, leasing can be considered an alternate source of funds—to short-or intermediate-term borrowings.

B. Recommended Methodology

Effective Cost of Leasing

The effective cost of leasing method involves identification of the differences, by annual period, between cash flows for the lease alternative versus cash flows for the purchase alternative. All cash flows are on an aftertax basis. The effective cost of the lease is the rate for which the net present value of these cash flow differences is equal to zero. This calculation is the same as that for the DCF internal rate of return method, used for investment analysis. The effective cost so determined is the rate which is paid for the funds provided by the lease. If this effective cost of leasing is higher than the firm's marginal after-tax borrowing rate (which periodically finances a purchase), it would be less costly to use funds raised through borrowing. The difference between the effective cost of leasing and the marginal borrowing rate is the financing premium, or savings, of leasing versus buying the asset.

Interest Cost on Funds Used for the Purchase Alternative

When analyzing the purchase option, the interest cost of funds provided by the firm should not be shown as a negative cash flow. The lease-buy analysis compares the cost of money for each alternative. If the lease cost of money is more than the marginal borrowing rate, the purchase option is less costly. To charge the purchase option with interest would be to penalize the cost of funds provided by the firm.

Impact on P and L

When comparing the impact of lease or buy on profit and loss, however, the interest should be reflected as a cost item under the buy alternative.

Other Considerations

In the analysis of lease-buy alternatives, it is desirable that like benefits be compared. If the items to be leased or purchased do not provide equal benefits, the difference in benefits should be quantified as accurately as possible. If they are not quantifiable, the premium for lease versus buy (or vice versa) will partially reflect different benefits and the decision to lease or buy must be made on subjective criteria. It is also important to compare alternatives using the *same number of periods* of cash flows. If the lease period is less than the life of purchased assets, an estimate should be made of the salvage or resale value of the purchased assets at the end of the lease period and the cash flow and salvage should be included for the purchase alternative. In this way, the two alternatives are made comparable in terms of periods of benefits and costs.

Exhibit 4: Methodology for Lease Versus Buy Analysis—A Diversified Manufacturing Company (continued)

C. Example

To illustrate the methodology described above, the following simple example is provided. The proposed lease would provide trucks with before-tax lease payments of $52.8M annually for the five-year estimated life of the vehicles. The equipment can be purchased at the end of the lease for a nominal amount by the lessee. The new equipment could be purchased for $176M as an alternative to the lease proposal.

Assumptions

An analysis of the lease-versus-buy option is detailed in the accompanying illustration. Operating costs for the vehicles are the same for each alternative, therefore they have been excluded from the analysis. Since the 10% ITC is passed through to the purchaser by the lessor, that can also be excluded. Except for the initial capital outlay which is expected at the beginning of the five-year period, it is assumed that all cash flows will occur continuously during each annual period; in the following analysis these cash flows are discounted using continuous discount factors. Sum-of-the-years' digits depreciation has been used for tax reporting purposes assuming a life of five years. The effective income tax rate used is 50 percent. Sales tax is paid by lessee whether lease or purchase is chosen.

Qualitative Aspects

It should be noted that the lease-versus-buy analysis is a quantitative tool and is only one of the considerations affecting the lease-buy decision. In many situations there will be qualitative factors which will influence the decision. These might include uncertainty of salvage value of purchased assets, risks of obsolescence, service provisions of leases, flexibility considerations, shortage of cash, etc. The qualitative aspects must be weighed against the relative costs of financing to reach a conclusion on the overall merits of the lease and purchase alternatives.

Lease or Buy Analysis After-Tax Cash Flows $000's

Year	Purchase Option Investment	Purchase Option Depreciation Tax Shield	Net Cash Flow (A)	Lease Option Lease Cost (B)	Difference (A)-(B)	Net Present Value @10 Percent	Net Present Value @11 Percent
0	$(176.0)	$—	$(176.0)	$—	$(176.0)	$(176.0)	$(176.0)
1	—	29.4	29.4	(26.4)	55.8	53.1	52.8
2	—	23.4	23.4	(26.4)	49.8	42.9	42.2
3	—	17.6	17.6	(26.4)	44.0	34.3	33.4
4	—	11.7	11.7	(26.4)	38.1	26.9	25.9
5	—	5.9	5.9	(26.4)	32.3	20.6	19.7
						1.8	(2.0)

Interpolating: $\frac{1.8}{3.8} = .5$

Effective After-Tax Cost of Leasing = <u>10.5%</u>

In this approach, the incremental after-tax cash flows of the purchase versus lease alternatives are analyzed. The cost of the funds provided under leasing is that discount rate which results in a net present value of zero for the incremental cash flows. In this example, the cost of funds provided by the lease is an after tax rate of 10.5 percent. If this rate is above the firm's marginal after-tax cost of borrowing (e.g., 5.0 percent), the purchase alternative would be preferred—from a cost of funds standpoint.

Table 2: Leasing Approval Authority in Participating Companies[1]

Decision Maker	Number of Mentions
Vice president-finance	24
Treasurer	19
Board of directors	10
Local managers	10
President	6
Director-financial programs	5
Assistant treasurer	4
Vice president-operations or administration	3
Management committee	3
Finance committee	3
Executive committee	3
Appropriatons committee	3
Real estate division	3
Controller	2
Planning department	2
Purchasing department	2
Corporate finance department	2
Capital expenditure committee	2
Other	5[a]

[1]Authority to approve varies with lease characteristics in 23 companies and is shared in 7 others.

[a]Includes one of each: Executive vice president, Policy Committee, Administrative Committee, Systems Advisory Committee, Budget Department.

committee must certify leases with aggregate payments ranging from $200 thousand to $500 thousand, and the board of directors must sanction all leases with total payments in excess of $500 thousand.

If power to authorize a lease is vested in a single individual or group, others are, as a rule, routinely involved. In a utility, for example, where the vice president of finance makes the decision, a leasing commitment is given only after a positive recommendation by the corporate economist. And in an airline, it is not unusual for a series of preliminary screenings to precede final lease approval by the full board of directors. An airline vice president and treasurer comments:

"After proposals have been solicited, received and analyzed, a presentation with the recommendations of the vice president and treasurer is submitted to the senior vice president of finance, vice chairman and executive vice president for approval. It then goes to the finance committee of the board of directors. Upon review and approval of the recommendations, it is forwarded by this committee to the board of directors for final approval."

Problems and Solutions

Most respondents indicate they have met with no significant problems in connection with their leasing activities. But 37 have encountered some problems of varying degrees of severity in connection with analysis, administration, control, delays or lessor inadequacies.

Analytical Difficulties

Analyzing lease offers has proven a demanding chore for some participants. Lack of consistency in the ways various prospective lessors submit bids—quoting different terms or renewal options, for example—makes comparisons among leasing proposals arduous. Other complicating factors include uncertainty about the residual values to include in the calculations made to determine whether to lease or buy, and on the weight to assign to qualitative influences in making decisions.

To deal with such impediments companies insist that, at a minimum, lessors provide precise answers to questions posed in bid requests. Freedom to be innovative in structuring deals is a privilege usually granted lessors, but only as an optional addition to complete responsiveness to the basic conditions set forth in solicitation correspondence (see pages 23-28).

Some cooperators depend upon the technique of sensitivity analysis to help them determine the significance of key variables. And the services of appraisers—usually external consultants but occasionally in-house experts—are sometimes used in efforts to gauge better the probable worth of the asset at the expiration of lease terms. Of course, a certain amount of subjective judgment is also brought to bear on the relative importance of considerations that resist quantification, such as the risk of obsolescence.

Administrative Burdens

Some find that the administrative burdens imposed on them as lessees are heavy. These concerns center on the substantial amount of paperwork and administrative support that leasing demands because of the exhaustive amount of accounting and economic analysis involved.

Shepherding the preparation by lawyers of especially complicated lease contracts (such as those for certain leveraged leases) had also proven a taxing chore for some lessees. Several volumes may be required to house the records: a basic contract; a participation agreement; two trust agreements—one each for lessor and debt participants; a purchase agreement; and perhaps some guarantees.

To compile these legal papers considerable input from lessees is usually called for. Many months (sometimes more than 12) may be needed to work out the wrinkles that arise in negotiations and reduce various agreements to a written form acceptable to all parties.

Because of the demands the documentation process places on management's time—and also because of the high cost that may attach to it (in rare instances attorneys' fees reach and even exceed $1 million)—a number of respondents have shied away from leveraged leases, preferring instead to rely on financing methods more quickly and less dearly wrought.

A unique and apparently persistent irritation posed by leasing is described by the treasurer of a chemical company:

"One of the more significant problems that we have found, having been involved in leasing in a material way over the last 20 years, is that when a business that employs leased assets is sold, a substantial amount of legal and administrative time is generated to convey the leased assets. In many instances, the corporation must still remain liable for the leased assets even though the new user is making the payments. In addition, even though the lease was capitalized on our balance sheet, and we still remain liable; in effect, we become a sublessor which still results in the asset being carried on our financial statements."

Control Problems

Divisions leasing to avoid corporate limits on capital expenditures, or to enhance their rates of return (because of the exclusion of leased assets from the investment base), are the main kinds of control difficulties faced by study cooperators commenting on the point. To combat them, these companies have either centralized control of the leasing function at headquarters, or modified applicable procedures to prevent implementation of uneconomic lease arrangements.

Delays

Various kinds of delays irk lessees. Specifically mentioned by several are those that sometimes arise in negotiations with lessors, especially on the details of leveraged leases, and in obtaining equity funds when this approach to leasing is employed. Less than timely presentation of lease documentation is another source of annoyance.

To reduce, if not eliminate such lags, most affected participants emulate the course of action taken by one of their number, a railroad, whose assistant vice president and treasurer describes it this way:

"We have dealt with it (delay) by initiating our activities on a transaction three months prior to the first equipment deliveries and keeping pressure on all parties to the transaction, particularly the lawyers, to keep the paperwork moving."

Lessor Deficiencies

Failure of lessors to perform up to promises is reported by two respondents. In one case, a leasing company representative proved unable to bring an agreed upon deal to fruition because his management would not go along with the terms he outlined. In another, the financial condition of a lessor prevented it from fulfilling its obligation under a lease. The remedy in both cases: Lessees looked elsewhere when arranging succeeding leases.

Chapter 3
Leveraged Leasing

LEVERAGED LEASING, a form of leasing that enables a lessor to obtain the entire tax advantages of ownership—namely, depreciation and investment credit—in return for only a partial investment in a leased asset, came into prominence during the 1970's. It is now often employed in connection with "big ticket" leases—those with payments accumulating to seven figure amounts or more. Forty respondents, or just over one-third of those surveyed, have obtained the use of such items as rolling stock, computers and aircraft through leveraged leases.

What accounts for the increased development of leveraged leases? An investment banker, whose firm acts both as a packager and investor in leveraged as well as straight leases—though seldom, if ever, as both in the same deal—believes a paucity of equity players constrained growth prior to 1970. Since then, more and more corporate and bank lessors attracted by the special tax-sheltering and profit-making potential of leveraged leasing have actively promoted it. And lessees in appropriate circumstances, have embraced it, as will be seen.

Characteristics

A leveraged lease is a tax-oriented finance lease that derives its designation from the position of the lessor in such a transaction. Rather than advance all the funds needed to acquire an asset to be leased, a lessor borrows as much as 80 percent of them from an unrelated source, and thus to a varying degree, depending upon the debt-to-equity mix reflected in the purchase outlay, leverages its investment.

Besides a lessor—the equity participant—and a lessee, a third party, a lender or debt participant, is, of course, essential to a leveraged lease. Usually the lender, often an insurance company, a commercial bank, or a pension fund advances funds on a nonrecourse basis; that is, it agrees to rely on the proceeds of the rentals, the security offered by the equipment, and the financial capacity of the lessee for repayment. Thus a lessor is relieved from any obligation related to the discharge of the indebtedness incurred to finance the purchase of the leased asset. However, its position would be subordinate to that of the lender in the event of a forced liquidation.

When a leveraged lease involves substantial amounts, intricate arrangements are sometimes required to bring the necessary parties together. Several equity and debt participants, as well as trustees, may be involved to represent their respective interests, by collecting and distributing rents and paying taxes, for example.

Why a Leveraged Lease?

For a lessee, one might expect that once a decision to lease is reached, its form would be of little consequence. This is not always the case, however. Many lessees favor leveraged leases because from experience they have found them to offer several advantages, not the least of which is lower cost than straight leases.

How can a leveraged lease prove less expensive? By leveraging, lessors conserve capital and increase returns—effects that enable them to be more aggressive in pricing lease proposals. And the substitution of a lessee's credit for that of a lessor's in third-party borrowing can also reduce costs if the lessee enjoys a better credit standing than the lessor and can, therefore, command a lower interest rate.

Besides offering savings, some lessees believe leveraged leases have better marketability than straight leases. (Many lessors prefer such arrangements not only because of the greater profit potential they promise but also because of the improved opportunity for diversification they provide. Instead of committing a substantial sum to a single straight lease, a lessor can invest the same amount in five distinct leveraged arrangements, or even more through syndication participations.) And a few lessees think they are able to negotiate better overall terms through leveraged leases because of the strong interest many lessors show in consummating them.

But despite the pluses that attach to leveraged leases, not all lessees find them attractive all the time. The complexity of many such arrangements makes the time necessary to complete them too much of a burden for some. For others the deals in which they are interested are unsuited to leveraged leases because of the relatively short periods involved. A few maintain it is quite difficult to work out acceptable tax indemnification provisions in leveraged leases (see accompanying box). And a couple mention that while the economics of leveraged leases makes them appealing, arrangement costs, including advisory and legal fees, sometimes prove too sizable an encumbrance. This is especially true where the total dollar amounts of lease payments are small. An investment official of a participating brewery notes, for example: "Leveraged leases are employed when the leased

Tax Indemnifications

To protect themselves from the adverse economic effects that would flow from the loss of depreciation, interest payment, or investment credit tax benefits, lessors often insist on the inclusion of tax indemnification clauses in lease agreements. Such provisions are typically designed to make them whole in the event tax advantages are lost for any reason. Formulas specifying the method of restoration may be spelled out in agreements.

Lessees, of course, seek to limit their tax indemnification risk. Often they will only agree to indemnify for losses they cause, not for those occasioned by lessors or resulting from changes in laws. Details on the tax indemnification positions lessees are willing to assume are often incorporated into solicitation letters presented to lessors.

equipment is sufficiently costly so that the benefits of cheaper capital (leveraged lease debt) outweigh the related increase in transaction costs."

Conformity with Internal Revenue Service Requirements

Lessors and lessees are vitally concerned about the income tax qualifications of the leveraged leases they enter. (Similar interest applies to straight leases, but may be less intense because of the generally smaller amounts involved.) Failure to comply with Internal Revenue Service (IRS) requirements would result in the loss of investment credit and depreciation benefits for lessors and of rent deductions for lessees—developments that would wreak havoc with any transaction intended as a lease.

To be absolutely certain that an arrangement designed as a lease is in fact a lease, the interested parties must obtain a Revenue Ruling from the IRS. Such a determination confirms that the arrangement will receive the tax treatment anticipated. (IRS procedure 75-21 details the filing requirements for Revenue Rulings in connection with leveraged leases.)

Since these rulings provide a foolproof method for ensuring the validity of tax assumptions in connection with leases, it might be assumed that such protection is sought automatically whenever a deal is arranged. But this is not the reality. While several consulted lessors insist on a Revenue Ruling as a sine qua non for the consummation of a lease arrangement, some lessees require that such findings not be absolute preconditions for the conclusion of agreements.

Why this dichotomy? There is no simple answer. But one plausible explanation is that lessees bear the brunt of lease-related fees and those of a legal nature for Revenue Rulings are

not insignificant. Another deterrent from a lessee's point of view is the lengthy time period—up to a year or more—needed to secure a finding from the IRS.

To obviate these problems, lessees may insist that lessors forego their insistence on Revenue Rulings and rely instead on opinions of counsel that lease arrangements will produce expected tax benefits. Or, more often, lessees may demand that conformity with the advance ruling guidelines, promulgated by the IRS in the drawing of leases, suffice. Generally, the tax guidelines as set forth in Revenue Procedure 75-21 require that, for a leveraged lease to qualify as such for federal income tax purposes, it meet the following conditions: The lessor must maintain an investment of at least 20 percent; the asset must have a specified minimum residual value (as much as 20 percent or more of cost) and useful life expectancy (at least one year) at the expiration of the lease term; the arrangement must produce a profit for the lessor; the lessee must be neither an owner nor a lender; the lessee or any related companies must not guarantee the third-party debt; and the lessor must assume some risk and not grant bargain purchase rights.[1] While the guidelines were designed expressly for leveraged transactions, many lessees and lessors are mindful of them even when negotiating straight leases.

The Investment Tax Credit

Section 38 of the Internal Revenue Code gives taxpayers the right to take credits against their federal income taxes for investments in certain kinds of assets. At present, 10 percent of the cost of the asset is the maximum credit allowed. It can only be claimed if the assets acquired have a useful life of seven years or longer. (Lower credits apply to assets with shorter lives but no credit is given for any asset with a useful life of less than three years.) The investment tax credit must be claimed for the first taxable year during which the assets are put into operation.

Lessors may retain the investment tax credit on leased assets or flow them through to lessees. The circumstances and desires of the two parties are the determining factors. Of course, lease rates reflect the disposition of the credit.

Lessee understanding of the investment tax credit and its workings is essential. Lacking that, accurate lease-versus-buy comparisons are impossible. In addition, lessees are sometimes asked to provide lessors with indemnifications against loss of the investment tax credit. Under such circumstances, total familiarity with Section 38 of the IRS code is essential to minimize the possibility of costly mistakes.

Packagers

When a company opts to use a leveraged lease, or even earlier—while contemplating what kind of financing to employ, for instance—it must decide whether to proceed alone or call on external packagers for assistance in making the necessary arrangements. Some turn the job over in its entirety to outsiders, while others share responsibility with them. Few, if any, lessees handle all the details themselves because they lack adequate in-house expertise or staffing in certain areas.

Many investment banking firms and commer-

[1]For detailed explanation and illustration of these requirements, see Richard M. Contino, *Legal and Financial Aspects of Equipment Leasing Transactions.* Englewood Cliffs, New Jersey, Prentice-Hall, Inc., 1979, pp. 209-220.

cial banks offer their services as packagers or arrangers of leveraged leases. Others, too, including independent leasing companies and brokers, are active as intermediaries.

How do companies choose among the many packagers available? The selection process often depends on the assignments prospective lessees intend to give the outside advisers. If complete responsibility is to be shifted, it is not unusual for a company to retain an investment banking house or commercial banking firm with which it has an established working relationship for other matters. However, if a packager is expected to fill a more limited role, its choice is often dictated by a contest (see below) among would-be representatives.

Duties

The duties assumed by a packager depend on the wishes of the prospective lessee and on its own orientation and capabilities. In some instances companies expect packagers to do virtually everything necessary to complete the financing. This can mean performing financial reviews, recommending for or against leasing, and making the arrangements—importantly, those related to design, and funding—if a decision to go forward with a leveraged lease is reached. The packager may even be expected to be the sole equity investor or one of several investors. In addition, packagers may be asked to line up debt investors, although several cooperators exempt them from this responsibility, hiring other intermediaries in their stead.

In other situations, packagers play a more limited role—that of equity underwriter. They do so on either one of two bases: firm or best efforts. If the former, packagers must be prepared to deliver equity money—which means they must have solid commitments from established capital sources, or possess the wherewithal to become investors themselves. If the latter, they need only make a serious effort to obtain the required funds.

Fees

Among packagers willing to discuss fees—not all were—there was general agreement that fees are negotiable and are often stated as percentages, ranging typically from about 0.3875 to 1.0 percent of the funds raised. The actual fee assessed depends on a number of factors, primarily: the amount involved and whether debt as well as equity monies have to be secured; the nature of the relationship between the client and the packager; and the workload. Thus a lessee might reasonably expect to pay a fee of from $75,000 to $200,000 to a packager for its contribution to the accomplishment of a $20 million leveraged lease.

Packaging fees are neither always easily determined nor especially important to lessees. According to an interviewed investment banker, intermediaries, such as his own firm, are sometimes asked to bid on an "all in" basis. This requires them to include their own fees together with those for other services (such as documentation) in the terms they quote customers. In such deals, gross fees may be set at 1.5 percent of the total financing amount, or thereabouts, and net fees (to the packagers) may exceed 1 percent if they are either able to place the deals advantageously or arrange nonunderwriting services inexpensively. If the total fees assessed satisfy lessees, their distribution is not a concern.

The charges of packagers are often contingent upon successful completion of the financing. In some instances, however, lessees are billed whether or not a leasing arrangement is consummated. This is almost always true where packagers act only as advisers and, after completing analyses, recommend courses of action other than leasing.

Arranging Leveraged Leases

Several options are available when companies decide to proceed with leveraged leases. Some simply select an equity source, perhaps the leasing subsidiary of a commercial bank with which a borrowing relationship exists, and ask for a proposal which they accept or reject when prepared. Others just ask a broker or independent lessor to make an offer. But most commenting lessees employ a screening approach in which prospecting and bidding precede the selection of a packager or lessor.

Preliminary Preparations

To launch their efforts to achieve an optimum leasing agreement, potential lessees, either independently or with the aid of outside experts, compile lists of prospective investors and packagers. Firms with which satisfactory past dealings have taken place and others that enjoy excellent reputations are included. Some simultaneously select investment bankers or others with private placement experience to raise the debt portions of the contemplated financings.

Competitions

As soon as likely investors or underwriters are determined, companies contact them to determine their interest and to attract proposals. The method described in the following comment by the manager of corporate finance of a utility is the one usually employed:

"Leveraged leases are primarily confined to computer equipment and are arranged on the basis of competitive bidding. In such cases, lease offers are solicited by the company through a mailing of detailed bid specifications to parties having previously demonstrated an interest in participating in such transactions."

Communications, commonly referred to as bid letters, serve as a basis for contests among interested lessors and lease underwriters. Normally these contain complete descriptions of the assets to be leased and their expected delivery schedule; details on the desired term, probable range of debt rates, and tax indemnification limits; posture on Revenue Rulings and IRS guidelines; and estimates of fees and other information helful to would-be bidders in shaping responses (see Exhibit 5). Several weeks are allowed for those interested in submitting replies, but cut-off dates are usually specified and adhered to.

Actual bids may be received from several interested lessors, while underwriting proposals of different kinds may be forthcoming from a few packagers. Responses indicate how long offers are open and what conditions apply—satisfactory completion of lease documentation is almost always one.

Exhibit 5: Bid Letter—Burlington Northern Inc.

FINANCE DEPARTMENT

176 East Fifth Street
St. Paul, Minnesota 55101
Telephone (612) 208-2121

January 27, 1978

I am attaching specifications with respect to a $45.7 million leveraged lease financing for seventy-one (71) new high horsepower (3,000 h.p.) locomotive units with deliveries scheduled for the second half of 1978. Forty-nine (49) of the units will be built by General Motors, Electro-Motive Division and twenty-two (22) by General Electric Corporation. The invitation to bid is being sent to a selected group of Brokers and Principals who have indicated prior interest in the transaction.

I have enclosed a list of officers and directors of the Railroad. This list should be used to verify that you or your affiliates have no interlocking officers or directors with the Railroad. I have also enclosed a copy of Burlington Northern's press release covering fourth quarter and twelve month 1977 results.

We would prefer that you adhere to the specifications set forth, however, alternative proposals will be evaluated on their respective merits. Any questions or requests for further information should be referred to my office. The proposals should be presented by Friday, February 17, 1978.

Very truly yours,

Assistant Vice President
Financial Planning

REQUEST FOR EQUIPMENT LEASE PROPOSAL

Burlington Northern Inc. (Railroad), hereby submits specifications for the purpose of soliciting financing proposals under a leveraged, investment tax credit lease for equipment identified in Section 1 below.

To assure that all standard lease proposals are submitted on a comparable basis, please adhere to the following guidelines and conditions:

1) Equipment

The equipment will consist of 71 new diesel-electric locomotive units as follows:

No. of Units	Type	Estimated Cost[2]
49	3,000 h.p. Model SD40-2 diesel-electric units, General Motors Company, Electro-Motive Division, manufacturer. Road Numbers BN 7063-7074, BN 7832-7868[1]	$31,119,900
22	3,000 h.p. Model C30-7 diesel-electric units, General Electric Company, manufacturer. Road Numbers 5545-5566.	14,570,600
71		$45,690,500

[1] BN will sublease 37 EMD units to the Colorado & Southern Railroad (BN subsidiary).
[2] Includes estimated freight charges.

It is planned to operate the locomotives in unit train coal service. All units will be equipped with "Pacesetter" controls (for lead position) which permits operation of locomotives at any increment of speed (0-15 mph) during loading and unloading of unit train coal cars; however, the units will not contain the lead control box.

All units incorporate the latest technical advances in design and will include:

— automatic fuel cut-off devices with pilot valve located in fuel tank.
— large capacity fuel tanks (4000 gallons).
— turbocharged engines.
— multiple unit control feature.
— automatic wheel slip control.
— solid state electrical excitation systems of modular design for ease
  in replacement and detection.
— dynamic brakes with 700 ampere capacity dissipating grids and built-in
  time delay relay for power to brake transfer.

— alternating current main generator.
— self-load test provisions to facilitate engine and electrical system
full load testing.
— large reinforced snowplow pilot.
— "anti-climb" nose with reinforced front cab design for safety purposes.
— extra ballast for heavy tonnage unit train service requiring maximum
adhesion.
— radio communication equipment; and rotating safety warning light.
— electric refrigeration; and recirculating lavatory facilities.

2) Estimated Schedule of Program and Settlement Dates

No. of Units	Manufacturer	Delivery Date(s)	Settlement Date*	Estimated Group Cost
20	EMD	July	July 25, 1978	$12,702,000
16	EMD	July-August	Aug. 15, 1978	10,161,600
18	EMD (13) GE (5)	October	Oct. 20, 1978	11,567,800
10	GE	Oct.-Nov.	Nov. 15, 1978	6,623,000
7	GE	November	Dec. 7, 1978	4,636,100
71				$45,690,500

*dates of deposit for debt funds are expected to coincide with settlement dates.

3) Term

Lease should provide for an initial lease period of sixteen (16) years, with the Lease Commencement Date estimated at January 3, 1979. Respondents should adhere to January 3 Lease Commencement Date unless Lessee advises that there is a valid commercial reason regarding equipment deliveries requiring an alternative date. The lease should allow for options to renew the lease (three, two-year renewal periods) or purchase at fair market value at the expiration of the basic lease period or any renewal thereof. No 'Puts' or lease extensions to third parties should be included in any proposal. Documentation with respect to this transaction should be completed prior to June 23, 1978.

4) Equity Contribution

Please indicate the percentage of equity to be contributed. Although the purchase price set forth in Section 2 is based on latest quotations from the manufacturers, your quotation should allow for an increase of up to 5% in total estimated group cost.

5) Debt Rates

Assume rates for long-term debt of 8%, 8-½% and 9%. Merrill Lynch Pierce Fenner & Smith Inc. will arrange for the long-term debt. While Railroad may elect to have a portion of the long-term debt serialized, Lessor(s) should use the rates provided in this section for the entire debt portion of the proposal. Should Railroad elect to have a portion of the long-term debt serialized, Lessor(s) will be expected to recalculate the lease rate factors so as to pass on to Railroad the resultant savings in interest expense. All units are expected to be delivered by December 31, 1978. The cut-off date for equipment will be June 30, 1979. In the case of units delivered after December 31, 1978 and before June 30, 1979, a recalculation of lease rentals will be permitted.

6) Structure of Lease

A. Base Term Rentals—State the seminannual lease rate factors and effective annual interest rates (implicit costs) for each long-term debt rate indicated in Section 5 above. All rates should be quoted *semiannually in arrears.* Proposals embodying other than level payment of rents per period will be entertained, and Railroad should be consulted with respect to such proposals prior to submittal.

B. Interim Rentals—Long-term debt and equity will be made available for each interim settlement date in proportion to the debt to equity ratio of the lease. It is desired that interim rent be paid by the Lessor(s). It should be calculated on the basis of interest only on debt taken down on interim settlement dates (as given in Section 2) calculated to Lease Commencement Date at the rates set forth in Section 5. In the event that settlement dates should vary from those set forth in Section 2, base term lease rentals will be recalculated. While it is believed that dates of deposit for debt funds and settlement dates for payments to manufacturers will be the same, variations may occur and the debt will be sold so that deposit dates may be changed by as much as four weeks from the dates set forth in Section 2.

C. Non-income Tax Indemnification—Railroad will indemnify against only non-income taxes such as sales, use and license taxes imposed upon the use of the equipment exclusive of Federal, state, local and foreign income, excise or franchise taxes.

7) Tax Indemnifications

Railroad's indemnification will be limited to the state and Federal income tax matters set forth below. Railroad will represent and warrant that the equipment will qualify as "new Section 38 property" within the meaning of the Internal Revenue Code of 1954 as of the time the equipment is accepted by Railroad. Railroad will not claim depreciation or investment tax credit with respect to the equipment. Railroad will represent and warrant that use of the equipment outside the United States will be de minimis. Railroad will indemnify Lessor after delivery and acceptance of equipment against loss of investment tax credit and accelerated depreciation caused by acts of commission or omission of Railroad. No other indemnifications will be provided. Adjustments in rentals (upward or downward) will be made if changes in the tax law (including investment tax credit) have been enacted and are effective as of Date of First Delivery of the equipment (est. at July 1, 1978) or if such changes are made effective on a retroactive basis to a date preceeding the Date of First Delivery. Proposals must disclose whether residual sharing is contemplated. Proposals which contemplate such sharing of residual will be disqualified from consideration unless regulatory clarification of this issue is made prior to date proposals are submitted.

8) Insurance and Casualty Values

Proposals should provide a schedule of casualty payment requirements (stipulated loss values) or the formula which would be used to compute such a payment. Railroad carries and maintains property damage and public liability insurance with respect to third party personal and property damage; however, Railroad reserves the right to maintain self-insurance with respect to property and to self-insure as to public liability with respect to personal and property damage at its option.

9) Operating Expenses

Railroad will be obligated for all costs associated with possession, control and operation of the equipment, including repair and maintenance expenses.

10) Commitment Letter

During the period prior to March 3, 1978, Lessor(s) will be asked to meet with representatives of the Railroad. At the meeting the Lessor(s) should be prepared to provide a Commitment Letter as to acceptance of the transaction, subject only to completion of satifactory documentation. Upon receipt of such Commitment Letter an award will be made.

11) Fees and Costs

All fees and costs including those of trustees are for the account of Lessor(s). Assume that fees for placement of debt will be 3/8 of 1% on the debt portion and $35,000 for printing and legal services. Cravath, Swaine & Moore, One Chase Manhattan Plaza, New York, N.Y. 10005, will represent the debt investors. Mercantile-Safe Deposit & Trust Company of Baltimore will act as Indenture Trustee. Assume the Indenture Trustee's fee will include an initial charge of $1000 and a fee of $50 per annum per investor.

12) Respondents

Railroad requires that proposals include the statement that the transaction has been or will be offered only to institutions and other sophisticated investors.

13) Potential Equity Investors

Enclosed is a list which sets forth the officers and directors of the Railroad. Lessor(s) should verify that equity sources or affiliates have no interlocking directors or officers with the Railroad. Should any equity investors(s) be in any such way related to the Railroad, such quotation will be withdrawn from consideration.

14) Reports

The Railroad will furnish customary annual reports with respect to the status of the equipment leased hereunder, and its published financial reports.

15) Rulings

Lessor may apply, if appropriate, to the Internal Revenue Service (IRS) for a Ruling as to the tax implications of the lease, but receipt of such Ruling should not be a requisite to execution of the documents. Railroad would prefer for administrative reasons that Lessor not require submittal of the lease to the IRS for a Ruling. Alternatively, the lease proposal may specify reliance upon Opinion of Counsel with respect to such tax matters and other provisions of the lease; or the proposal may specify that reliance on neither such Ruling nor Opinion of Counsel is required. Proposals must conform *in all respects* to IRS Technical Information Release 1362, April 11, 1975, on Rev. Proc. 75-21 and 75-28 setting forth guidelines for advance rulings "Leveraged Lease of Property".

16) Submittal of Proposals

Lease proposals and inquiries should be submitted to Burlington Northern Inc.:

Proposals must be submitted to this office no later than February 17, 1978. All proposals should state the date and time of expiration, but in no event should expiration be earlier than March 3, 1978.

17) Acceptance of Proposals

Railroad reserves the sole right to accept or reject any or all proposals and need not accept a proposal solely on the basis of its having the lowest present value cost. With respect to proposals submitted by lease underwriters, the Railroad does not require that "firm money" be part of the proposal. However, within an appropriate time period, to be determined at the discretion of Railroad, subsequent to February 17, source(s) of equity must be made known to Railroad. On proposals which meet the other qualifications herein and which have no difference between effective cost to Railroad, preference will be given to that proposal which can advise at the earliest possible date of the source(s) of equity that will be party to the transaction.

BURLINGTON NORTHERN INC.

Selection

Bids or proposals are first reviewed to ensure consonance with the requirements outlined in the solicitation letters. This done, those that conform are subjected to a financial analysis, and ordinarily the low bidder is then awarded the deal. (Bids not responsive to all specifications are usually rejected outright.)

In the event that the successful bidder is a lease underwriter bidding on a best-effort basis, a reasonable amount of time is granted for it to produce the equity investment (and the borrowed funds if a different investment banker or other representative has not been assigned this responsibility). To assist in attracting equity and debt funds, underwriters often prepare information packets for prospective investors and lenders. Those for equity investors typically include computer printouts of cash flow, amortization schedules, and tax payments, as well as summaries of debt and depreciation assump-

tions, and of potential investment yields. Those for lenders are somewhat akin to the offering circulars used in connection with private placements; they contain financial and background information designed to facilitate analysis by potential debt holders.

If, for any reason, the chosen packager is unable to complete the financing by a fixed date, the award is ordinarily rescinded. Another contestant is picked, perhaps the low bidder among investors or packagers that have entered firm underwriting proposals.

After the competition winner is finally determined, some companies ask their attorneys to take charge and bring the lease to fruition. A few, however, get in touch with the selected equity source and ask for a commitment letter, confirming details of the proposed lease before calling in counsel. They believe this step helps eliminate any last-minute snags that might cause an almost certain transaction to come apart.

Chapter 4

Lessee Experience with FASB Statement No. 13, Accounting for Leases

HISTORICALLY, the information that companies furnish to the public about leasing arrangements was largely confined to sketchy footnotes to their financial statements. Adoption of Financial Accounting Standards No. 13, "Accounting for Leases," (henceforth referred to as FAS 13), brought an end to this practice. It was issued by the Financial Accounting Standards Board (FASB)—the designated private-sector rule-making body on accounting matters—in November, 1976. While FAS 13 and its subsequent amendments and interpretations pertain to both lessors and lessees, emphasis here is given to its impact on lessees.[1]

Lessee Accounting and Reporting

FAS 13 requires that lessees classify all leases at their inception as either capital or operating

[1] Amendments to FAS No. 13 include: FAS No. 17, Accounting for Initial Direct Costs; FAS No. 22, Changes in the Provisions of Lease Agreements Resulting from Refunding of Tax Exempt Debt; FAS No. 23, Inception of the Lease; FAS No. 26, Profit Recognition on Sales-Type Leases of Real Estate; FAS No. 27, Classification of Renewals or Extensions of Existing Sales Type or Direct Financing Leases; FAS No. 28, Accounting for Sales with Lease-Backs; and FAS No. 29, Determining Contingent Rentals. Interpretations of FAS No. 13 comprise: FAS No. 19, Lessee Guarantee of the Residual Value of Leased Property; FAS No. 21, Accounting for Leases in a Business Combination; FAS No. 23, Leases of Certain Property owned by a Governmental Unit or Authority; FAS No. 24, Leases Involving Only Part of a Building; FAS No. 26, Purchase of a Leased Asset by the Lessee During the Term of the Lease; and FAS No. 27, Accounting for a Loss on a Sublease. A comprehensive publication incorporating the standards section of Statement 13, as amended and interpreted, is now available from the Financial Accounting Standards Board, Stamford, Connecticut.

leases. Capital leases accomplish one or more of the following: provide for a transfer of ownership to the lessee at the conclusion of the term; contain a less-than-fair market value purchase option; cover a term that is 75 percent or more of the asset's approximated economic life; reflect at inception a present value of the minimum lease payments of at least 90 percent of the fair market value of the leased assets. Operating leases do not meet any of these criteria.

How a lessee must account for a lease under FAS 13 depends on whether it is a capital or an operating lease. Generally, a capital lease must be recorded as both an asset and an obligation in an amount equal to the present value of the total of minimum lease payments, exclusive of any executory costs to be paid by the lessor. And fair market value of the leased asset must be recorded whenever it is less than the amount determined by the present value computation.

A lessee must amortize a capital lease in accordance with rules that apply to the various capitalization tests. If, for example, ownership passes to the lessee at the end of the term, or a bargain purchase option applies, the leased asset must be written off in the manner the lessee normally employs for assets it owns. However, if either of the other two criteria for capitalization prevails, the asset must be amortized, in keeping with customary practice, over the term of the lease to the value projected for it at the lease's conclusion.

Different rules apply to operating leases. Usually payments under such arrangements must be charged as expenses when they fall due. Even if actual rental payments are not uniform in amount, they should be recognized on a straight-line basis. But, in the event that another systematic and rational approach is more representative of the time pattern in which use is derived from the leased asset, it should be employed. For example, lease payments for manufacturing equipment could be expensed on a units-of-production basis, provided it is possible to make a reasonable approximation of the total units to be produced during the lease term.

Several utilities indicate that, as regulated companies, they are conforming with the requirements of FAS 13 by following the provisions set forth in the addendum to the Accounting Principals Board (APB) opinion No. 2, "Accounting for the 'Investment Credit'," to account for leased assets. But this may soon change. Earlier this year, the FASB announced it was considering new rules that would alter the lease accounting methods now prescribed for regulated enterprises such as utilities—by permitting lease capitalization, for instance.

Disclosure Rules

FAS 13 requires that lessees disclose specific information on lease arrangements in their financial statements or in footnotes to these statements. Assets recorded under capital leases, as well as the accumulated depreciation and related obligation, must be separately identified. So must the applicable amortization charge, unless it is included with depreciation expense and this is stated. In addition, the following disclosures are required in connection with capital leases: a general description of leasing arrangements; the gross amount of assets recorded under capital leases; the future minimum lease payments; the total of minimum sublease rentals to be received in the future under noncancelable subleases; and the total contingent rentals actually incurred for each period for which an income statement is presented (see accompanying box). Require-

ments for operating leases include disclosures of rental payments in addition to a general description of arrangements and minimum future lease payments.

Impact of FAS 13

Speculation was rife when FAS 13 was issued concerning the unmanageable effects it might have on lessees. Some thought the directive to capitalize certain leases might prompt many companies subject to it to abandon leasing. Others worried lest suddenly swollen debt-to-equity ratios induced by the implementation of the statement would cause adverse reactions by lenders, investment managers, and stockholders. Judging from the experience of respondents, these fears were largely, though not totally, misplaced.

Inconsequential Influence

Most commenting lessees (55) indicate that the new accounting rules have neither markedly influenced their approach to leasing nor otherwise affected their business. Many of them state that leasing accounts for such a small percentage of their total capital needs that the burdens imposed by FAS 13 are insignificant—mainly the loss of off-balance sheet financing and an increase in accounting and administrative chores. None of these lessees reports encountering any problems with lenders or other investors as a result of the implementation of FAS 13. This suggests, not surprisingly, that such parties possessed sufficient savvy to incorporate leasing information into their credit and investment decision making prior to the promulgation of the statement.

Of course, another largely unstated but possible explanation for FAS 13's lack of influence on many lessees may lie in the ease with which its strictures—particularly those on capitalization—can be circumvented. Consider, for instance, a lease that must be capitalized because the 90 percent criterion applies. Negotiations and adjustments can provide a way around this requirement—by reducing the present value of lease payments to 88 percent of the asset's fair

Examples of Disclosure of Lessee Capitalized Leases

MELVILLE CORPORATION (DEC)

Consolidated Balance Sheets

	1978	1977
Property, plant, equipment and leasehold improvements, at cost:		
Land	$ 2,214,581	$ 2,083,987
Buildings	17,921,175	16,805,782
Machinery and equipment	11,055,967	10,739,619
Store and office fixtures, improvements to leased properties and miscellaneous equipment	211,657,640	178,878,118
	252,849,363	208,507,506
Less accumulated depreciation and amortization	113,462,891	97,561,210
Net property, plant, equipment and leasehold improvements	139,386,472	110,946,296
Deferred charges and other assets.	2,352,952	2,001,126
Leased property under capital leases, net of amortization (note 8)	29,696,864	22,242,244
Goodwill (note 2)	29,117,669	29,875,034
Current liabilities:		
Accounts payable and accrued expenses	$160,111,323	$143,443,891
Federal income taxes	18,237,778	14,996,884
Current installments on long-term debt	6,023,150	6,011,444
Current installments of obligations under capital leases (note 8)	902,843	640,316
Total current liabilities	185,275,094	165,092,535
Long-term debt	40,653,137	46,673,987
Obligations under capital leases (note 8)	33,177,215	25,151,422
Deferred Federal income taxes	4,116,891	3,358,062
Lease obligations for closed stores.	3,677,571	2,649,470
Minority interest in subsidiaries	41,640,623	34,300,285

Consolidated Statements of Changes in Financial Position

Source of Funds:		
Net earnings	$ 87,987,472	$ 73,148,197
Expenses not requiring outlay of working capital:		
Depreciation and amortization:		
Fixed assets owned	20,421,961	17,539,306
Leased property under capital leases	1,667,306	1,193,683
Amortization of goodwill	757,365	711,514
Minority interest in net earnings	21,589,176	16,928,522
Increase in deferred Federal income taxes	758,829	2,045,001
	45,194,637	38,418,026
Working capital provided from operations	$133,182,109	$111,566,223

Note 8: Leases—The Company and its subsidiaries lease various retail stores, warehouses, plant and office facilities generally over periods ranging from 5 to 25 years with options to renew such terms from 5 to 15 years.

In 1978, the Company changed its policy of accounting for capital leases to comply with the provisions of Statement of Financial Accounting Standards No. 13—Accounting for Leases. As a result, certain leases previously classified as operating leases have been accounted for as capital leases. Accordingly, the present value of future minimum lease payments under such leases has been recorded as leased property under capital leases, net of amortization (computed on a straight-line basis over the life of the lease), and obligations under capital leases. Rent expense, interest expense (reflected in cost of goods sold and store operating, selling and general and administrative expenses) and Federal income taxes have been retroactively restated to reflect this change.

The change resulted in decrease in 1978 net earnings of $457,552 or $.02 per share. The retroactive application of the change resulted in a restatement of 1977 net earnings to reflect a decrease of $262,090 or $.01 per share. For years prior to 1977, the effect of the retroactive application of the change decreased retained earnings at December 31, 1976 by $1,353,608.

Leased property under capital leases includes:

	1978	1977
Retail facilities	$12,218,315	$ 9,896,389
Warehouse, plant and office facilities	26,166,730	19,366,730
	38,385,045	29,263,119
Less accumulated amortization	8,688,181	7,020,875
	$29,696,864	$22,242,244

At December 31, 1978, the future minimum lease payments under capital leases, rental payments required under operating leases, and the future minimum sublease rentals are as follows:

	Capital Leases	Operating Leases
1979	$ 3,955,826	$ 54,670,583
1980	3,947,426	55,108,655
1981	3,926,058	52,414,332
1982	3,914,658	50,074,149
1983	3,914,658	47,558,970
Thereafter	53,575,737	342,953,445
Total	73,234,363	$602,780,132
Less amount representing interest .	39,154,305	
Present value of minimum lease payments	$34,080,058	
Total future minimum sublease rentals		$ 4,797,585

The following schedule shows the total rental expense for all operating leases:

	1978	1977
Minimum rentals	$54,976,413	$ 48,840,943
Contingent rentals	80,268,559	69,673,010
	135,244,972	118,513,953
Less sublease rentals	788,808	802,394
	$134,455,164	$117,711,559

Contingent rentals consist primarily of rentals for leased shoe departments operated under license agreements with K mart Corporation. These license agreements are for a term of 25 years and provide for rent payments based upon sales with additional rentals based upon profits. The agreements also provide for the maintenance of certain performance standards based on sales and profitability which become operative commencing with the eleventh year of the agreements. Remaining contingent rentals relate to other Company operations and are based only on sales. Contingent rentals under capital leases amounted to $274,044 in 1978 and $222,855 in 1977.

THE BFGOODRICH COMPANY (DEC)

	1978	1977
	($000)	
Current Liabilities		
Current debt......................	$ 30,435	$ 28,104
Accounts payable and accrued expenses	371,901	303,314
Currently payable income taxes	23,964	35,121
Current portion of capitalized lease obligations	5,238	7,684
Current sinking fund requirement—		
Series A Preferred Stock....	1,260	—
Total Current Liabilities	432,788	374,223
Non-Current Obligations		
Funded debt	411,176	410,086
Capitalized lease obligations	65,382	67,715
Deferred income taxes	85,188	75,955

STATEMENT OF ACCOUNTING POLICIES

Property and Depreciation—Property is recorded at cost, with depreciation and amortization thereof, including amounts for capitalized leases, computed principally by the straight-line method.

NOTES TO FINANCIAL STATEMENTS

(Dollars in thousands, except per share amounts)

Long-Term Lease Commitments—Goodrich and its subsidiaries conduct certain operations in leased facilities, primarily tire centers, warehouses and office buildings, and also lease certain manufacturing facilities and machinery and equipment.

The data presented below is in accordance with the Financial Accounting Standards Board Statement No. 13, "Accounting for Leases."

At December 31, 1978 and 1977, property recorded under capitalized leases was as follows:

	1978	1977
Land	$ 58	$ 58
Buildings	54,827	52,679
Machinery and equipment	42,640	54,840
	97,525	107,577
Allowances for depreciation and amortization	36,600	38,481
Total Property........................	$60,925	$ 69,096

The future minimum lease payments by year and in the aggregate, under capitalized leases and under noncancelable operating leases with initial or remaining noncancellable lease terms in excess of one year, consisted of the following at December 31, 1978:

	Capitalized Leases	Noncancelable Operating Leases
1979	$ 11,449	$ 17,813
1980	10,206	15,056
1981	9,294	12,646
1982	8,407	10,022
1983	8,013	8,429
Thereafter	90,121	36,729
Total minimum payment due........	137,490	$100,695
Executory costs	694	
Amounts representing interest......	66,176	
Present value of net minimum lease payments	70,620	
Less current portion of capitalized lease obligations	5,238	
Total	$65,382	

Net rent expense on operating leases was $22,335 in 1978 and $21,723 in 1977, after deducting sublease rentals of $5,431 and $5,107, respectively.

Minimum future sublease rentals to be received on capital and operating leases amounted to $7,034 and $12,848, respectively, at December 31, 1978.

Source: "Accounting Trends and Techniques—1979," American Institute of Certified Public Accountants, New York, N.Y.

market value, for example, thus producing an operating rather than a capital lease. Some observers believe many lessees are taking advantage of the loopholes in FAS 13. For example, a partner in a public accounting firm spoke with reference to the 90 percent criterion: "It's hard for anyone to identify, but I would say there are 500 who avoid it to every one that capitalizes leases."[2] Supporting this contention is the statement of a participating rubber company executive on the capital-lease reporting criteria:

"These are technical barriers which will be removed. New leases will skirt or avoid capitalization under the new accounting rules."

Meaningful Effects

Eleven survey respondents state that FAS 13 has materially influenced their attitudes or postures on leasing. Most of them now lean toward buying assets when operating leases cannot be arranged. One, the director of financial planning of a diversified manufacturing company, expresses a representative view: "A lease does not typically receive favorable consideration if on-balance sheet capitalization is required unless it includes characteristics not available through purchase." Disclosure avoidance is not the sole impetus for such positions. Some shun leases that might be capitalized out of fear of violating covenants in outstanding loan agreements bearing on maintenance of stipulated working capital positions or financial ratios.

A few companies have turned their backs on smaller leases because they find complying with the statement's requirements onerous. Even where leases have been evaluated and found economically attractive, they are rejected because of the workload involved in classifying and accounting for them.

Two companies are changing the hurdle rates they employ in certain of their lease-versus-buy

[2]*Barrons*, March 17, 1980.

analyses as a result of the implementation of FAS 13. Instead of comparing the lease rate with that for borrowing, as they used to, they are comparing it to an unspecified but higher rate—one they believe compensates for the freshly perceived additional advantage, off-balance sheet financing, still offered by operating leases. Thus, for some, a lease financing at 12 percent might, under some circumstances, be preferred to owenership via a bank loan at 10 percent.

Marginal Effects

An indirect effect of the statement, felt by several companies, relates to its impact on financial statement analysis. Opinion is about equally divided as to whether it helps or hinders in attempts to evaluate performance vis-a-vis that of competitors or to measure results achieved by various underlying units. Here are two contrasting views.

"It has provided a means for a more meaningful comparison of our company's results with those of our peers."

Manager-domestic financing,
an automotive parts company

*   *   *   *

"The people in our Controller's Division, who have worked closely with FAS No. 13, believe that it has resulted in noncomparable financial statements among companies (and even among operating units within companies) since some companies have been able to structure leases in a way which does not require capitalization, while other companies have capitalized similar leases."

Executive vice president,
a chemical company

Recommendations for Revision

"We believe that the new rules are generally needed and acceptable," says the vice president and controller of a metal products manufacturer. This view of FAS 13 is shared by most respondents. Only 31 participants voice displeasure with the statement as it now stands and offer suggestions for its improvement.

Elimination of Loopholes

Several companies express irritation over the ease with which many of those subject to the statement are able to flaunt its requirements. They want the loopholes closed. One common recommendation: Do away with the classification system and mandate the capitalization of all leases.

Simplification

About a dozen respondents find FAS 13's rules either too complex or too murky. They complain not only about the detailed computations required by the statement and its various amendments and interpretations, but also about the absence of needed definitions or illustrations—on materiality and "take or pay contracts," for example. What is needed, some of these companies maintain, is a thorough overhaul of the standard that will produce an uninvolved, easily followed directive. Others see a need for a more limited revision. Substitution of a single, term-based criterion for the four existing norms presently governing lease capitalization would satisfy them. Typical suggestions appear in the following statements:

"As we have indicated to the Financial Accounting Standards Board, we are concerned regarding the ever-increasing complexity of financial accounting requirements relating to the accounting for leases. With the extensive number of published and proposed amendments and interpretations to the already complicated Statement No. 13, administration of lease-accounting activities has become increasingly difficult and the possibility of misinterpretation or misapplication of standards has expanded significantly.

"We urge a thorough review of Statement No. 13, including all its amendments and interpretations, with the objective of developing a single comprehensive standard."

Executive vice president,
a steel company

*   *   *   *

"We would prefer a simplification of FAS No. 13 whereby all leases over some period (for example, three or five years) would be classified as capital leases and all leases for shorter periods would be classified as operating leases."

Director-treasury division,
a chemical company

Removal of Uncertainties and Inconsistencies

A few respondents are troubled by the flow of statements complementing FAS 13, as well as by the number under consideration.[3] Putting a stop to this flux would, in their estimation, go a long way toward removing the uncertainties now faced in accounting for leases.

A handful of surveyed lessees express discontent over the lack of consistency in the statement. For example, several point out that it is possible for the same transaction to be treated for accounting purposes as an operating lease by the lessee and a sale by the lessor and still be in compliance with FAS 13. (Nothing requires agreement between the parties on what the finance charges are. Consequently, each is free to provide its own interpretation of how the lease transaction conforms to the 90 percent criterion on capitalization.) And a couple cite what they perceive as the standard's erratic posture on the recognition of inflationary influences. Voicing annoyance and appealing for

[3]In late 1979, the FASB decided not to issue statements relative to exposure drafts on Estimates of Residual Values by Lessors and Lessees, and Lessees' Use of the Interest Rate Implicit in the Lease.

improvement, one participating financial executive offers this comment:

"In some respects recent accounting rules attempt to reflect 'economic reality' (i.e., the substance of the transaction) rather than simply recording the 'form' of the transaction. However, in other respects the rules fall back on historical accounting form and ignore substance (or economic reality). For example, a recent FAS proposal about Statement No. 13 requires that inflation expectations be ignored in the determination of residual values. Yet, elsewhere, FAS No. 13 requires the application of current incremental borrowing rates which clearly include an inflation expectation component. We would welcome the development of accounting rules which are theortetically consistent. . . ."

Repeal

"Ideally we would recommend elimination of the rules. They seem to have created more problems than they have solved for us." This sentiment, expressed by the vice president-corporate planning and treasurer of a machinery manufacturer, is unique in that it is the sole suggestion offered by cooperators calling for total repeal of FAS 13. However, four others lend partial support to this position by advocating recision of certain of the norm's provisions. Two recommend that lessees not be required to estimate implicit lease rates, or lessors' at risk residuals as now alternatively prescribed under the 90 percent criterion; and two urge withdrawal of the capitalization requirements—in their entirety in one instance and partially (the 90 percent criterion) in the other.

Chapter 5
Outlook

MOST LESSEES offering an opinion believe their dependence on leasing over the next five years will vary relatively little. But, as the tabulation below indicates, among those expecting change, more look for an increase than a decline.

Anticipated Five-Year Leasing Trend	Number of Mentions
Steady	45
Up	20
Uncertain	14
Down	4

Continuance of Status Quo

Of companies that anticipate steadiness in their leasing habits, some simply state that their policies or guidelines discouraging leasing are not expected to change, and so neither will their usage. Along similar lines, others cite the foreseen absence of increased opportunities to employ leasing profitably. A chemical company executive, for example, puts his prediction this way:

"We do not expect to materially increase or decrease our reliance on leasing in the future because we do not expect the relative advantage of financing through lease or ownership to change significantly."

Two others see conflicts between policies favoring leasing and strictures imposed by FAS 13 producing standoffs that will contribute to maintenance of the status quo. And a utility forecasting a level trend maintains that financing considerations preclude any growth in the use of leasing. The manager of corporate finance explains:

"We have a primary objective that total leases will not exceed 5 percent of capitalization. We feel that leasing in excess of this amount would be adversely perceived by our rating agencies. For this reason, leases are evaluated and selected on a discriminating basis within that 5 percent of capitalization framework. Because of our close adherence to this limited lease objective, we do not expect to increase our reliance on leasing as a financing vehicle over the next five years."

Growth Forecasts

Twenty lessees predict they will increase their use of leasing during the first half of the 1980's. Many of them point to ambitious spending programs coupled with capital shortages as the reason for their forecasts. For example, the treasurer of a glass manufacturing firm, which had a compound annual sales growth rate in excess of 20 percent during the 1970's, makes this forecast:

"I presently believe that we will increase our reliance on leasing during the next five years. This assumes that our capital needs will continue to accelerate and that the cost of leasing will continue to be less than the opportunity cost of having to forego some expansion of our business."

Several growth predictions flow from respondents' beliefs that greater emphasis on leasing will enable them to reap rewards not available through purchasing. Some, especially those with stretched-out construction plans, see leasing as easing cash flow pressures. Others

---

Another Leasing Spur

Tax-exempt financings are often tied in with leases. A municipality, for example, may sell industrial revenue bonds to finance a plant that will attract an employer to the area. Although title to it ordinarily resides in the governmental body issuing the bonds, the facility is built to the specifications of the prospective employer. To ensure retirement of the indebtedness, the company using the facility leases it from the debt issuer with rentals arranged to provide for debt repayment.

Several respondents indicate they intend to enter leases linked to such financings at intervals in the future, just as they have in the past. Lower cost than that available through conventional financing is the primary spur. (The tax-free status of interest payments on industrial revenue bonds permits their issuance of relatively low coupon rates—a condition that translates into lower-than-normal lease rates.) Of course, the fact that a custom-built facility may be made available at a reasonable price when the debt is retired is another inducement.

Several respondents point out that except for pollution control financings, where no cap applies, $10 million is the limit on the amount of capital outlays a company may finance in any jurisdiction through industrial revenue bonds. Because of this constraint, leases are sometimes arranged to augment those related to tax-exempt financings. For example, a project requiring $15 million for completion might be funded via a $10 million industrial revenue bond financing and a separate $5 million lease negotiated with a nongovernment lessor.

---

view leasing as an excellent means of coping with the threat of obsolescence. Several retailers with expansionary ideas consider leasing the most fitting way to finance their new locations. And two participants indicate that exceedingly stiff competition among lessors holds forth the promise of increasingly attractive deals for lessees.

Uncertain Future

Fourteen questioned lessees are unsure whether their use of leasing will change markedly during the next several years. Most of them maintain that unpredictable circumstances affecting the appeal of leasing will tip the scales one way or the other, or leave them balanced.

Here are a few representative comments in this vein:

"We do not have any expectations in terms of the degree to which we will utilize leasing in the future. . . . We review the leasing option on a situation-by-situation basis and make the decision based on financial and operational advantages and disadvantages."

Vice president and controller,
a drug company

* * * *

"We would expect to increase our reliance on external financings as our capital and exploratory expenditures for new petroleum and alternative energy supplies increase more rapidly than our ability to fund them through our traditional internally generated sources of funds. Whether we lease or finance via other third-party means depends upon the relative economics of the two alternatives. The maintenance of lessor-lessee tax rate disparities is a prerequisite of future beneficial leveraged lease economics."

Treasurer,
a petroleum company

* * * *

"Our reliance on leasing during the next five years will depend on the availability of attractive lease terms during that period. I cannot predict at this point the volume of our leasing activity.

Treasurer,
a retail company

Contraction Prospects

The four respondents that look for a near-term decline in the volume of leasing they transact offer several reasons for their prognostications. One lessee, believing a contraction in its growth rate is imminent, intends to cut back on leasing in favor of "less expensive financing approaches." Another thinks leasing will be less compatible with its future financing requirements because it anticipates a diminished need "for the type of equipment suitable for leasing over the next five years as contrasted to the past five years."

A third mentions the increased administrative costs and impairment of financial ratios induced by FAS 13 as the basis for its projection. And the final forecaster of declining usage indicates that the surrender of residual values necessitated by leasing will probably lead to a de-emphasis of this financing technique, especially in light of its expectation of rampant inflation.

Appendix

Because the Board's basic research report in this field, "Leasing in Industry," Studies in Business Policy, No. 127, 1968, is out of print and only a few loan copies remain available, it was deemed appropriate to include a number of still relevant excerpts from that study here. While the interest rates quoted in certain of the case studies may remind readers of the halcyon days of yore, the examples remain valid—only the numbers need be changed. Indeed, a continuance of the downward trend in rates in evidence at the time of this writing could make the illustations appear of recent vintage.

Examples of Items Leased

Real Estate
Airplane hangars
Office space and office buildings
Gasoline service stations
Manufacturing space and ready-to-operate factories
Retail stores
Warehouses and warehouse space

Office Equipment
Card-punching and card-sorting machines
Computers
Duplicating machines
Furniture
Typewriters

Industrial Equipment for:
Air conditioning
Construction
Electronic production and control
Machine tool manufacturing
Material handling
Roadbuilding

Transportation Equipment
Airplanes
Airport refuelers
Automobiles and trucks
Fire engines
Railroad cars
Tankers
Trailers
Yachts

Machinery for:
Bottle capping
Canning
Metalworking
Packaging
Printing
Power generating
Shoemaking
Textile manufacturing

Miscellaneous Items
Dairy cattle
Harbor dredges
Offshore drilling platforms
Pipelines
Showcases
X-ray equipment

Negotiating a Lease and Selecting a Lessor

In drafting the terms of a lease arrangement or in negotiating about a lessor's proposal, a lessee must keep in mind the following considerations:

• The nonfinancial services the lessor will provide and their value to the lessee
• The financial impact of the lease (which is influenced by the implicit interest in the lease payment, the disposition of residual values of the leased assets, any deposits or advance payments the lessor may require, the lessor's willingness to share any portion of the investment credit to which it is entitled, and the timing and level of lease payments)
• Arrangements for renewing the lease or for purchase options
• Cancellation privileges
• Possible tax problems (under certain circumstances tax authorities interpret leases as conditional sales contracts or loan agreements).

If two or more lessors offer equally acceptable terms, the choice among them may be dictated by an advantage that only one of them can provide—for instance, avoiding the participation of third parties in the lease contract—or by some intangible factor such as reputation.

* * *

Criteria Suggested by a Lessor for Selecting a Lessor

When lessors are asked what criteria lessees should use in selecting a leasing company, the considerations most frequently mentioned are experience, reputation, professional skill, knowledge of the facilities to be leased, and reputation for favorable terms. Some leasing companies emphasize the importance of technical services. Others, like the lessor who suggests the following criteria, stress finanical considerations:

1. The lessor should be adequately capitalized.

2. It should be experienced and stable.

3. It must comply with all legal and tax requirements of the states in which it operates.

4. It should be willing to execute a firm commitment to lease (provided that mutually acceptable documentation is obtained), and not a commitment contingent on the lessor's ability to secure underlying financing.

5. It should deal directly with the lessee rather than through a broker.

6. It should be willing to make a full disclosure of its financial condition.

* * *

Difficulties in Comparing Rates Charged by Professional Lessors

When the rates offered by lessor organizations rest on different bases, it is frequently difficult to compare them. For large lease transactions with top-rated companies, leasing rates usually are quoted in terms of simple or actuarial interest, i.e., interest per annum on the unamortized balances. Professional lessors often refer to this rate as a standard and call it, for example, "7% simple." It is, however, more usual for leasing companies, particularly in the field of equipment leasing, to employ an "add-on" rate. An add-on rate is one that is applied to the gross acquisition cost or initial value of the leased equipment for the full term. The charge thus obtained is added each year to the amount required to pay back, or amortize, the principal. While the add-on rate applies to the total amount financed, lease payments reduce that amount gradually to zero. Thus the average amount of the outstanding principal of the lease is approximately half the initial outlay, and the quoted add-on rate, which appears low, must accordingly be roughly doubled to be equivalent to a simple interest rate applied annually to unamortized balances. For example, a 6.0% add-on rate on a 48-month lease is equivalent to a 11.0% simple interest rate.[1]

Varying requirements of advance payments and uneven payment schedules sometimes further complicate the comparing of quotations submitted by different leasing companies. Advance payments, for instance, commonly range from one month's rental to twelve months'.

However quoted, rates offered by a single leasing company often shift according to the credit-worthiness of the lessee. A lessee with a very high credit rating is likely to be offered an effective interest rate from less than 1 to 1½ percentage points in excess of the prevailing prime borrowing rate; to a good but not top credit risk, the typical offer may be 2 percentage points or more above the prime rate; companies with lower credit ratings frequently pay 12% to 14% simple interest when they lease.

The rates listed in published rate cards or brochures of leasing companies are in most cases intended to apply to finance-type equipment leases written for the small or medium-sized lessee. They are generally expressed in terms of dollars per month rather than percentages. Many lessors say they prefer to illustrate leasing costs in this way so that the lessee may quickly compare the monthly dollar costs of owning equipment and of leasing it. Some concede that another reason is to avoid showing the equivalent high simple interest rates.

The following is a comparison of charges quoted by several well-known leasing companies per $1,000 of equipment for a period of five years, assuming that the investment credit is passed through to the lessee. The approximate add-on rates and the equivalent simple interest rates have been computed to facilitate comparison. As the footnotes to the table indicate, the companies have differing advance-payment requirements, none of which are reflected in these rates; neither are nonfinancial services offered by individual companies, nor the loss of residual values.

Leasing Company	Total Leasing Costs		Approximate Rates	
	Per Month	60 Months	Add-on	Simple
Aˣ......	21.70	1302.00	6.0%	10.9%
B•......	22.00	1320.00	6.4%	11.5%
C⁺......	22.50	1350.00	7.0%	12.5%
D•......	23.00	1380.00	7.6%	13.5%
E*......	23.33	1400.00	8.0%	14.1%

x Amount of advance payment depends on type of equipment and credit rating of lessee
• No advance payment required
+ Advance payment of 5 months required except for top-rated lessees
* Advance payment of 6 months required

[1] Rates are from tables in "Financial Rate Translator and Guide to Legal Instalment Sales Rates," issued by the Financial Publishing Company, Boston, Massachusetts.

Evaluating a Lease Proposal

The proper evaluation of a lease proposal by a prospective lessee requires determination of whether the company is primarily concerned with the nonfinancial services offered, with the financial impact of the lease, or with the profit potential of the leased facilities. Depending upon which of these is the overriding consideration, a variety of background data must be gathered, such as:

• The estimated purchase cost of the property to be leased, its expected economic life, and its expected residual value
• The tax effect of allowable depreciation on the property
• The company's current interest rate for direct borrowing, its estimated over-all cost of capital; and its anticipated return on alternative investment opportunities
• What it would cost the company to perform, itself, the operating services offered by the lessor.

The nonfinancial services a lease provides include: (1) operating and administrative services—for example, maintenance, insurance protection, record keeping, payment of property taxes, engineering advice and other counsel, and intangibles such as saving the time of the lessee firm's management; and (2) where applicable, protection against obsolescence of the leased facilities.

A typical approach to estimating the cost of nonfinancial services is to subtract from the lease payments the estimated components covering depreciation of the lessor's investment and interest. The resulting difference can then be compared with what it would cost the lessee to perform, itself, those services it actually requires.

The financial impact of leasing is usually measured either in terms of an effective rate of interest paid for lease financing or in terms of total cash outlay for leasing compared with cash outlay for owning and borrowing. These approaches are particularly useful when the need and economic justification for the facilities have already been established and when the problem is accordingly the selection of the most advantageous method of acquiring their use.

Some companies find it desirable to evaluate leases by determining the rate of return attributed to the profit-making or cost-saving potential of leased facilities. They therefore make an analysis of the economics of a direct investment to determine whether ownership is acceptable, and then make a similar analysis to see if leasing would have comparable profit potential.

Both in the evaluation of financial impact and in the measurement of profit potential, two basic approaches are employed. One, a short cut, deals with averages and is quite simple to carry out. The other, much more involved, takes into account the time value of money and shows the present-day values of future cash outlays and receipts.

* * *

Compensation for the Lessor's Nonfinancial Services

The minimum service any lessor performs is to finance the use of facilities for a lessee that would otherwise have to obtain them with its own funds or through some form of loan. Many lessors perform services such as maintenance and record keeping in connection with the facilities they lease. And lessors of electronic data-processing equipment and industrial machinery typically offer another nonfinancial service: protection, in the form of cancellation privileges, against the risk of obsolescence.

If the lessor submits a lease proposal, compensation for its nonfinancial services is generally buried in the gross lease payments; very few lessors itemize this charge. The lessee's negotiator can, however, estimate it by taking the difference between the lease payments and the sum of (1) the depreciation charges it would have if it purchased the asset, and (2) interest charges applied to undepreciated balances. Should it be desirable to divide this estimate into a component for operating services and a component reflecting protection against the risk of obsolesence, the lessee can calculate the cost it would incur if it performed the operating services itself or had an independent concern do so. This cost is then subtracted from the estimated total charges for the lessor's nonfinancial services to arrive at the premium paid for protection against obsolescence.

The procedure is usually reversed when the lessee's negotiator is structuring the lease. He first makes an estimate of how much his company would have to pay for performing needed operating and administrative services. Then he adds to this the amount he deems to be fair compensation for insurance against obsolescence. Finally, he adds to the total (1) either depreciation charges or reduction of principal payments

on an equivalent direct loan, and (2) appropriate interest charges.

*　　*　　*

Evaluating Obsolescence Protection

Many users of EDP equipment and expensive industrial machinery seek to avoid the danger of early obsolescence of the equipment resulting from (1) its inability to meet future demands that will be much greater or more complex than their present demands; or (2) the availability of new equipment that will fill their needs much more rapidly or far less expensively. They are therefore willing to lease such equipment and pay what amounts to an insurance premium for the privilege of canceling leases before termination, rather than own the equipment and face the prospect of having to dispose of it well before it had paid out.

To appraise the risks of obsolescence, and thus help to reach sound lease-or-buy decisions, answers are sought to such questions as:

• How long before the equipment under consideration will become obsolete in terms of its capacity or capability?
• What arrangement can be made with the lessor for canceling the lease before termination?
• What would be the costs (e.g., reprogramming in the case of computers) of converting to equipment of higher capacity or greater capability when such equipment becomes available, and what would be the potential gain foregone, in terms of operating efficiency or systems improvements, of delaying the acquisition of such equipment?

Quite a few companies that own their computers or industrial machinery take an occasional look at the price they would have to pay to get protection against the risk of obsolescence in a short-term cancelable lease. They get one or more lease quotations and then deduct from the quoted rentals what it would cost them to own (including financing costs) and service the equipment. The remainder of each lease payment is presumed to cover, for the most part, protection from the risk of obsolescence. The premium the user would pay as lessee is sometimes regarded as the *saving* to the owner for retaining the risk of obsolescence.

Estimation of the premium for protection against obsolescence is simplifed if the firm has a maintenance and service contract for owned equipment. It merely adds the annual costs of the contract to the estimated borrowing and depreciation costs that are applicable to the purchase price, and deducts the total from the annual payment called for in a lease proposal.

Whether or not they own EDP equipment or industrial machinery, some firms weighing lease-versus-buy decisions make a "breakeven" analysis to establish when after-tax rental costs will exceed net purchase costs (investment outlay and after-tax operating costs less tax benefits on depreciation). The rationale of the method is that continued use of owned equipment or machinery once it becomes inadequate in capacity or efficiency would be prohibitively expensive; therefore, the penalty of buying equipment that becomes functionally obsolete is the excess of accumulated net purchase costs (less salvage value) over accumulated net rental payments made up to the time a trade-in becomes imperative.

Break-even Analysis of Buying *vs.* Leasing a Computer

A pharmaceuticals manufacturer

The management of this company analyzed the practicability of buying the two-year-old computer that it was renting under a cancelable lease. It used two bases of comparison. The first assumed that the present computer would have to be replaced in a year and a half by a computer of greater capability and capacity. The second involved an estimate of how long the company would have to own the computer to break even financially with continued rental.

The probable trade-in or resale value of the present equipment after a year and a half was the largest unknown factor in the first comparison. Assuming a "worst possible" case of zero trade-in value and a "best possible" case of 30% trade-in on the manufacturer's original selling price, a computation indicated that if the equipment were purchased for $838,200, the net after-tax total additional cost—as compared with renting—would range from $225,000 ("worst possible"), or $66,000 ("best possible"). Either way, purchase appeared to be unattractive.

The second basis of comparison established a year-by-year, after-tax net cost of ownership compared with leasing. In this analysis no attempt was made to take into account the time value of the money required to buy the equipment. The calculations showed that a payout or break-even point would not be reached until a little more than three years after the purchase, and that after five years the cumulative cash advantage of purchasing would be $251,000. But since even three years was regarded as too long a time to wait for replacement of the computer, management concluded that purchasing it would not be practical. The conclusion was reinforced by three other factors that management considered unmeasurable but important:

1. The probability of a poor or almost nonexistent resale market for this type of computer at the time the company would dispose of it

2. The possibility of rental reductions as industry competition heightened

3. Reluctance to take on maintenance of the computer.

DETAILS OF CALCULATION

Following are the basic financial data and assumptions on which the analyses were made. The two tables labeled Basis No. 1 and Basis No. 2, giving both the first and second methods of analysis, are on page 48.

Basic Financial Data and Assumptions on Computer Rental and Purchase

Annual computer rental....................	$369,300
Cost of buying computer from lessor.........	838,200
(82% of the manufacturer's selling price when new)	
Income tax rate..........................	48%

The company planned to take straight-line depreciation on the computer if it purchased it. But in line with established policy covering new assets, only half the annual depreciation charge would be taken during the first year ownership.

The company also planned to continue renting the tape drives of the computer—their rental accounted for $86,000 of the total annual rental of $369,300. In addition, it would have, as owner, outlays for maintenance, insurance, and local taxes. The following schedule shows the estimated annual charges for these items and for the tape-drive rentals for the first five years of ownership:

Year	Maintenance, Local Taxes, and Insurance (1)	Continued Rental of Tape Drives (2)	Total (Columns 1 & 2) (3)
1..............	$10,200	$86,000	$96,200
2..............	10,200	86,000	96,200
3..............	32,900	86,000	18,900
4..............	24,300	86,000	110,300
5..............	16,900	86,000	102,900
Total book expense, 5 years	94,500	430,000	524,500
Total cash flow after income tax..........	49,100	223,600	272,700

Basis No. 1—Net Additional Cost to Purchase and Replace Equipment after 1½ Years

Ownership	Book Entry (Charge)/ Credit (1)	Net Cash Flow after Tax In/(Out) (2)	Rental Net Cash (Outlay) after Tax (3)	Additional Cash (Costs) from Ownership (Col.2-Col. 3) (4)
(A) Assuming zero trade-in or resale value				
Year 1				
1. Capital cost	$(838,200)	$(838,200)		
2. Maintenance, insurance and other costs	(96,200)	(50,000)		
3. Depreciation: at $558,000 per year (½ in 1st year)	(279,400)	134,100		
4. Net result for year 1 (1 + 2 + 3)		(754,100)	$(192,000)	$(562,100)
First half of year 2				
5. Maintenance, insurance, and other costs	(53,200)	(27,700)		
6. Depreciation and write-off of remaining book cost	(558,800)	268,200		
7. Net results for first 6 months of year 2 (5 + 6)		240,500	(96,000)	336,500
8. Cumulative totals for 1½ years (4 + 7)		(513,600)	(288,000)	(225,600)
(B) Assuming a 30% trade-in or resale value				
Year 1				
9. Capital Cost	(838,200)	(838,200)		
10. Maintenance, insurance and other costs	(96,200)	(50,000)		
11. Depreciation: at $354,600 per year (½ in 1st year)	(177,300)	85,100		
12. Net results for year 1 (9 + 10 + 11)		(803,100)	(192,000)	(611,100)
First half of year 2				
13. Maintenance, insurance and other costs	(53,200)	(27,700)		
14. Depreciation write-off of remaining book cost	(354,600)	170,200		
15. Realized from salvage value	306,300	306,300		
16. Net results for first 6 months of year 2 (13 + 14 + 15)		448,800	(96,000)	544,800
17. Cumulative totals for 1½ years (12 + 16)		(354,300)	(288,000)	(66,300)

Basis No. 2—Break-even Analysis of Purchasing or Owning

End of Year	Ownership Costs				Rental Net Cash (Outlay) after Tax (Cumulative) (5)	Additional Cash (Costs) from Ownership (Cumulative) (Col. 4-Col. 5) (6)
	Maintenance, Insurance, Local Taxes and Tape Drive Rental (Cash Charge) (1)	Depreciation (Noncash charge) (2)	Net Cash Flow In/(Out) After Tax			
			Current Year (Col. 1-48% [Col. 1 & Col. 2]) (3)	Cumulative (4)		
0 (Investment)			$(838,200)	$(838,200)		$(838,200)
1	$(96,200)	$(139,700)	17,100	(821,100)	$(192,000)	(629,100)
2	(96,200)	(279,400)	84,100	(737,000)	(384,000)	(353,000)
3	(118,900)	(279,400)	72,300	(664,700)	(576,000)	(88,000)
4	(110,300)	(139,700)	9,700	(655,000)	(768,000)	113,000[1]
5	(102,900)	—	(53,500)	(708,500)	(960,000)	251,500
Total	(524,500)	(838,200)	(708,500)	—	—	—

[1] Break-even point would be reached early in the fourth year, when, even if the equipment had no salvage value, the owner's $88,000 unrecovered investment would be largely offset by a tax benefit of 48% of the equipment's undepreciated book value of $139,700.

A Discounted-Cash-Flow Method of Calculating the Rate of Lease Financing for a New Plant

A diversified manufacturer

This company planned to build a manufacturing plant on a site, acquired sometime previously, that was currently valued at $45,000. The total cost of the plant was estimated at $1,857,000. The construction would take place in three stages over a five-year period, according to the following schedule:

Period	Work Accomplished	Outlay
End of 1st year	Original unit completed and put into operation	$697,000
End of 3rd year	First addition completed and put into operation	560,000
End of 5th year	Second addition completed and put into operation	600,000
Total outlay		$1,857,000

Citizens of the area where the plant was to be located offered to arrange lease financing of the plant through a local foundation they had created to encourage new industry. The essentials of their proposal were:

• The company would sell the land to the foundation.
• The foundation would supply the company with funds on the three-stage schedule indicated above.
• The company would make annual payments of irregular amounts (see column 1 of the table on page 50) that over a 24-year period would amortize the total construction costs, cover the foundation's administrative costs, and yield the foundation-lessor a modest annual return on its funds.
• Although the company could terminate the lease after 24 years, it could renew the lease for another 16 years at a greatly reduced annual rental

and, after that interval, at a still more favorable rental.

To evaluate this proposal, the company calculated the rate of lease financing, using the discounted-cash-flow method. In this calculation it assumed that if it owned the plant it would take depreciation over the 40-year period on a double declining basis. The year-by-year results are shown in the table.

The net funds flow or tax adjusted lease payments (column 5 of table) were such that a 2.35% after-tax rate of lease financing equated them to a total present value approximately equal to the investment cost less the present value of the remaining worth of the property after 40 years (column 6). When converted to a before-tax basis, this rate was lower than the company's borrowing rate of 5%. In other words, leasing appeared to be attractive compared with ownership by borrowing. The rates were sufficiently close that management also weighed other considerations (e.g., the community relations value of leasing through the local foundation, and the possibility of an eventual loss of control over a strategically valuable site) before reaching a decision.

IMPACT OF RESIDUAL VALUES

The company notes that if it had chosen to discount the estimated residual value loss of $324,975 at a value-of-capital rate of, say, 10% after tax, instead of at an after-tax rate of lease financing of 2.35%, the present value of the loss would have been only about $7,149 instead of approximately $121,030 (column 6). On this basis, the remaining present value of $1,894,851 ($1,902,000-$7,149) would have been equated to the stream of tax-adjusted lease payments totaling $2,365,416 (column 5) at a rate of approximately 2%, instead of 2.35%, or at a before-tax rate of lease financing of about 4% rather than 4.6%.

This shows that the loss of residual value at the end of a lease, particularly a long-term lease, assumes decreased current importance to the lessee, and its penalty against the lease is measurably lessened, if residual values are viewed as an uncertain future loss resulting from taking a calculated business risk rather than as an obligatory final "payment" made to obtain lease financing.

Evaluation of Proposed Lease of Manufacturing Plant by Determining Implicit Rate of Lease Financing

Year	Total Lease Payment (1)	Depreciation if Owned (2)	Net Lease Cost (Excess of Lease Cost over Depreciation) (Col. 2)-(Col. 1) (3)	Net Tax Benefit of Leasing (48% of Col. 3) (4)	Net Funds Flow (Tax-adjusted Lease Payment) (Col. 1-Col. 4) Total (5)ª	Pres. Val. @ 2½% (6)
0	($45,000)ᵇ				($45,000)	($45,000)
1	$59,599	$36,450	$23,149	$11,112	48,487	47,304
2	59,599	34,470	25,129	12,062	47,537	45,246
3	104,894	60,590	44,304	21,266	83,628	77,657
4	104,894	57,435	47,459	22,780	82,114	74,395
5	153,422	84,450	68,972	33,107	120,315	106,346
6	153,422	80,130	73,272	35,180	118,242	101,960
7	153,422	76,020	77,402	37,153	116,269	97,817
8	153,422	72,140	81,282	39,015	114,407	93,894
9	153,422	68,460	84,962	40,782	112,640	90,191
10	153,422	64,960	88,462	42,462	110,960	86,682
11	153,422	61,645	91,777	44,053	109,369	83,350
12	153,422	58,625	91,797	45,503	107,919	80,249
13	153,422	55,735	97,687	46,890	106,532	77,278
14	153,422	53,015	100,407	48,195	105,227	74,469
15	153,422	50,425	102,997	49,439	103,983	71,800
16	153,422	47,955	105,467	50,624	102,798	69,245
17	153,422	45,555	107,867	51,776	101,646	66,802
18	153,422	43,385	110,037	52,818	100,604	64,507
19	153,422	41,275	112,147	53,831	99,591	62,294
20	153,422	39,270	114,152	54,793	98,629	60,183
21	97,022	36,245	60,777	29,173	67,849	40,397
22	97,022	34,435	62,587	30,042	66,980	38,909
23	51,728	32,705	19,023	9,131	42,597	24,140
24	51,728	31,075	20,653	9,913	41,815	23,120
25	5,000	29,525	(24,525)	(11,772)	16,772	9,047
26	5,000	28,045	(23,045)	(11,061)	16,061	8,451
27	5,000	26,640	(21,640)	(10,387)	15,387	7,900
28	5,000	25,310	(20,310)	(9,479)	14,479	7,253
29	5,000	24,050	(19,050)	(9,144)	14,144	6,912
30	5,000	22,845	(17,845)	(8,566)	13,566	6,467
31-40	50,000	174,160	(124,160)	(59,597)	109,597	45,724
Total	3,116,238	1,597,025	1,564,213	772,694	2,365,416	1,704,989
Residual value	—	—	—	—	$324,975ᶜ	121,030
Total discounted value	—	—	—	—	—	1,826,019
Total investment cost (incl. land)	—	—	—	—	—	$1,902,000

(The present value of the Net Funds Flow discounted at 2½% is less than the total investment cost. Hence, another trial rate (2%) was used, and by interpolation, the effective lease financing rate was found to be 2.35% after tax or about 4.6% before tax.)

ª Column 5 is equivalent to 52% of lease payment plus 48% of depreciation.
ᵇ Represents sale of land to the foundation.
ᶜ Of this sum, $259,975 represents the value of the plant (the initial investment of $1,857,000 minus accumulated depreciation of $1,597,025, per Col. 2) and $65,000, the estimated value of the land after 40 years.

Use of Average Annual Costs to Obtain a Discounted-Cash-Flow Rate of Lease Financing

A major international oil company

This company gives the following description of how it evaluated a proposed long-term tanker charter:

PROBLEM DEFINITION

"As its long-range tonnage requirement indicates that an additional tanker is needed, a foreign affiliate proposes to lease for 20 years a 65,000-ton tanker rather than construct and own a like tanker. The vessel could be time-chartered for 20 years for an annual charter payment of $1.3 million that would include the services of a crew and maintenance. Estimated cost of constructing such a vessel is $6.15 million, and basic annual operating costs (wages, provisions, insurance, repairs, and overhead) would be approximately $5 million. Straight-line depreciation ($308,000 per year), and a 50% tax rate are applicable.

BASIS FOR ECONOMIC EVALUATION

"Since there is no question as to the need for additional tonnage and since chartering is essentially an alternative to direct borrowing to finance ship construction, a comparison should be made of the cost of financing a vessel by means of chartering and by direct borrowing. The comparison can be effected by determining the discount rate which equates the after-tax cash flows resulting from a decision to charter instead of own. This discount rate will be the effective after-tax interest cost inherent in the charter and should be compared with the affiliate's usual after-tax borrowing rate."

The following table shows how the evaluation was made.

Annual charter cost.....................	$1,300,000
Less: average annual value of operating services furnished........................	500,000
Net charter cost before tax...............	800,000
Less: income tax........................	400,000
Net average annual charter cost after tax...	400,000
Plus loss of tax benefit on depreciation (50% of $308,000).........................	154,000
Net after-tax cost to lease in excess of own...	$ 554,000

It was determined by use of interest tables that $6,150,000 the cost of the tanker, is the present value of an annuity of $554,000 per year for 20 years when money has a value of 6.4%.[1] Therefore, the effective *after*-tax interest rate inherent in the charter is 6.4%. This was compared with the affiliate's after-tax borrowing rate of 4.5%; and the company also took into account other considerations, such as the prevailing investment climate.

---

[1] *Details of Calculations:*
If $6,150,000 = present value of $554,000 per year for 20 years at X%, dividing each side of equation by $554,000:

$11.101 = present value of $1 per year for 20 years at X%,

Per interest tables:

$11.241 = present value of $1 per year for 20 years at 6¼%.
$11.018 = present value of $1 per year for 20 years at 6½%.

Interpolating:

$11.101 = present value of $1 per year for 20 years at approximately 6.4%.

A Discounted-Cash-Flow Analysis of the Financial Rate of Return Gained by Owning rather than Leasing a Computer

A diversified manufacturer of consumer and industrial products

This company usually finds it more economical to rent its electronic data-processing equipment than to buy it. An exception occurred, however, when it examined the merits of buying a $1,130,000 computer installation it was then leasing. The examination, which involved a discounted-cash-flow analysis of the financial rate of return, showed a 13% after-tax return in favor of purchase. Details of the analysis and the underlying assumptions appear on the table on page 52. As a supplementary step, the break-even point for ownership was estimated (see "Net Cash Flow" column in the table).

Discounted-cash-flow Analysis of Financial Rate of Return Obtained by Owning Rather than Leasing a Computer

Year	Savings (Note 1)	Maintenance (Note 2)	Insurance (Note 3)	Net Cash Savings	Less Income Tax Effect (52%) (Note 4)	Savings after Taxes	Tax Savings from Depr. (Note 5)	Total Net Cash Savings	Purchase Price, Sales Tax, and Salvage Amounts (Note 6)	Net Cash Flow (Note 7)	Present Value of Cash Flow at 13%
0 Purchase Price									1,130,548	(1,130,548)	(1,130,548)
0 Sales Tax									56,527	(27,133)	(27,133)
1	480,000	40,000	2,600	437,400	227,448	209,952	111,160	321,112	—	321,112	284,184
2	480,000	40,000	2,600	437,400	227,448	209,952	111,160	321,112	—	321,112	251,462
3	480,000	40,000	2,600	437,400	227,448	209,952	111,160	321,112	—	321,112 Payout	222,563
4	480,000	40,000	2,600	437,400	227,448	209,952	111,160	321,112	—	321,112	196,938
5 (Incl. Salvage)	480,000	40,000	2,600	437,400	227,448	209,952	111,160	321,112	(61,704)	382,816	207,793
Total	2,400,000	200,000	13,000	2,187,000	1,137,240	1,049,760	555,800	1,605,560	1,125,371	509,583	5,259

(Financial rate of return on investment is approximately 13.0%)

Notes:

1. *Savings*—Represents the amount being paid as rental (including maintenance and insurance) plus sales tax. $39,942 per month × 12 = $479,304 annual amount (rounded to $480,000).

2. *Maintenance*—Cost of proposed maintenance contract at present included in rental fee. $3,320 per month × 12 = $39,840 annual amount (rounded to $40,000).

3. *Insurance*—Cost of insurance at present included in rental fee. $217 per month × 12 = $2,604 annual amount (rounded to $2,600).

4. *Income tax effect*—Savings are comparable to income. We will, in effect, pay 52% of savings as income tax.

5. *Tax savings from depreciation*—Equipment becomes depreciable assets when purchased.
   Assumptions made are: Use straight-line method of depreciation: purchase price less salvage value is used as basis; and depreciation period is 5 years.
   $1,068,844 net cost ÷ 5 Years = $213,769 annual depreciation charge.
   $213,769 × 52% Tax Rate = $111,160 annual cash benefits through reduced tax liability.

6. *Sales tax*—5% × $1,130,548 = $56,527
   Sales tax is an allowable item of expense; therefore only 48% of the tax amount represents a net cash outflow.
   $56,527 × 48% = $27,133

7. *Payout or break-even point*—3.6 years.

It was recognized that the estimated return of 13% reflected *only* the financial advantage of purchasing rather than leasing the computer. This return, of course, would be in addition to any return expected from economies to be achieved by using the computer.

Management believed that two factors other than those included in the analysis pointed to the desirability of buying, rather than continuing to lease, the computer. First, one advantage of leasing over owning—that leasing made feasible rapid conversion to better electronic data-processing equipment as it came on the market—did not obtain in this instance. There was a strong likelihood that the computer would be adequate to the company's needs for a long time, and the risk of obsolescence before the break-even point was thought to be minimal. Furthermore, even if this risk were severe, because of the inflexibility of the machine language used in the existing computer, the company would have to undertake very expensive reprogramming if it replaced it.

Second, the $61,704 estimate of the salvage value of the computer was considered to be very conservative; it might well run to five times that amount, in the company's opinion.

CASE STUDY 5 ||||||||||||||||||||||||||||||||||||||||||||||||||||||||||||||||||||||

A Discounted-Cost-of-Acquisition Analysis for Evaluating Three Alternative Methods of Financing a Plant

An industrial equipment manufacturer

The company was offered an opportunity to acquire a $1,400,000 plant in a desirable area. A local development agency submitted two lease proposals for financing this facility, which would be built and fully equipped according to the company's specifications:

1. *A conventional 20-year lease:* Total lease payments would be made at a uniform level of about $103,000 over the 20-year life of the lease. These payments would retire the lessor's 4% bonds that would provide the funds under this arrangement, but would not cover property taxes which the company would pay separately.

2. *A purchase-type 20-year lease:* The lessee would pay the same amounts as above but would treat the lease as a purchase and take an owner-borrower's tax deduction for depreciation and interest at 4%.[1]

While evaluating the lease proposals, the company examined the feasibility of a third alternative: outright purchase with borrowed funds at 5% interest, and principal reductions to be at a uniform level of $10,000 a year for 20 years. Under both the outright purchase alternative and the purchase-type lease, the company would fully depreciate the plant buildings, worth $1,000,000 over 40 years, and the equipment, worth $400,000 over 12 years.

DETAILS OF CALCULATION

The company evaluated the three alternatives by making a discounted-cost-of-acquisition analysis covering a 40-year period in order to reflect the full impact of (1) income tax allowances on depreciation available to an owner over the entire life of the plant, and (2) the lower property tax cost to the company as lessee when title is held by a local development agency.

Disposition of residual values did not have to be reflected in this analysis; for if the company chose either leasing alternative, the lessor would agree either to transfer the property to it for a nominal sum at the end of the lease or to renew the lease at a nominal rental.

Management had previously established that the after-tax value of capital to the company was, depending on the risk involved, between 5% and 20% (*vs.* after-tax borrowing costs of about 2½%). Accordingly, to supply several bases on which to make a judgment, the net cash flows, after 48% tax, associated with each of the three financing alternatives were discounted at four rates: 5%, 10%, 15%, and 20%. The calculation was carried out by means of a standard computer program. A summary of the results follows:

---

[1] The purchase-type lease is actually an instalment purchase contract put into lease form for the convenience of the parties (in this case, to permit the agency to continue to hold legal title), but allowing the lessee to take tax deductions, generally with clearance by the Internal Revenue Service, on depreciation and equivalent interest.

Formula for Determining Net Cash Flow	Cash Flow (In thousands of dollars)				
		Discounted			
	Total	5%	10%	15%	20%
1. Conventional lease: .52 lease payments + .52 property tax...	$1,160	$706	$478	$351	$273
2. Purchase-type lease: Principal + .52 interest + .52 property tax − .48 depreciation..........	1,160	675	425	288	209
3. Outright purchase: Principal + .52 interest + .52 property tax − .48 depreciation..........	1,287	795	538	392	302

On the basis of this analysis, the company chose the purchase-type lease. It pointed out that, of the two leasing alternatives, the purchase-type lease was the more favorable because the combination of tax benefits on equivalent interest and depreciation it could take as an owner, although the same in total for the 40-year period as the total tax deductions on the conventional lease, had a timing advantage attributable to accelerated depreciation. As the tabulation shows, moreover, the higher the value of capital to the company, the more attractive the purchase-type lease in comparison with the conventional lease.

CASE STUDY 6 |||||||||||||||||||||||||||||||||||||||||||||||||||||||||||||||||||||

Use of a Financial Model Analysis to Evaluate the Sale and Leaseback of an Office Building

A large manufacturing company

This company planned to erect a new office building at a cost of $450,000 on a site occupied by an obsolete building. The book value of the land was $20,000; of the existing building, $60,000. Abandonment of the old building would produce a tax credit of $30,000 (50% of $60,000) if the company continued to own the property. Because the company's commitments under its capital expan-

sion program limited its borrowing opportunities, management contacted two lessors to see what arrangements could be made for a sale-and-leaseback transaction. One lessor offered an arrangement that was more attractive than that proposed by the other, and that in fact had an interest-cost component that compared favorably with the company's own prime borrowing rate. To make sure that this sale-and-leaseback proposal was as economically desirable as borrowing the money to build and own the building, the company compared these two alternatives by means of a financial model analysis.

THE ECONOMIC DATA

The economic data on which the analysis was based were as follows:

Under the *sale-and-leaseback proposal:*

• The lessor would buy the land and building for $100,000. Thus the company would pay a capital gains tax of $5,000 (25% of $100,000 over $80,000 book value for the land and building).[1]

• Of its total investment of $550,000 ($100,000 for the land and building, $450,000 for the erection of the new building), the lessor would amortize $410,000 through its leasing charges over a 25-year period.

• At the end of this period, the company would make a balloon payment of $140,000 to exercise a purchase option for the property.

• Predicated on a 4¾% interest rate, these payments would be $34,760 a year: $28,110 to amortize and pay interest on the $410,000, and $6,650 annual interest on the remaining $140,000 represented by the balloon payment.

Under the *ownership option:*

• The company's net cash investment to own the new building would be only $420,000: $450,000 less $30,000 tax credit on the write-off of the old building. But its actual net *economic* investment would be $515,000 because, under ownership, it would forgo the $95,000 net proceeds from the

---

[1] The cost of dismantling the old building was not taken into account in the analysis, since the company would incur this cost under either alternative.

Office Building—Lease vs. Own
(Owner Investment of $515,000 at 5% vs. Lessor Investment of $550,000 at 4¾%)

	Lease	Ownership via Borrowing—at 5%				Lease vs. Own	
Year	*(1)* Annual Lease Cost After Tax	*(2)* Cash Investment Beginning of Year	*(3)* Interest Cost After Tax 2.5% of (2)	*(4)* Tax Savings from Depreciation (45-Year DDB on 450,000)	*(5)* Annual Cash Cost to Own (3) − (4)	*(6)* Total Annual Cash Advantage to Own (1) − (5)	*(7)* Cash Investment End of Year (2) − (6)
Building cost, $450,000—tax credit, $30,000		$420,000					
Proceeds of sale, $100,000—$5,000 capital gain tax		95,000					
0	$17,380ᵃ						$515,000
1		515,000	$12,875	$10,000	$2,875	$14,505	500,495
2		500,495	12,512	9,555	2,957	14,423	486,072
3		486,072	12,152	9,130	3,022	14,358	471,714
4		471,714	11,793	8,724	3,069	14,311	457,403
5		457,403	11,435	8,337	3,098	14,282	443,121
6		443,121	11,078	7,966	3,112	14,268	428,853
7		428,853	10,721	7,612	3,109	14,271	414,582
8		414,582	10,365	7,274	3,091	14,289	400,293
9		400,293	10,007	6,951	3,056	14,324	385,969
10		385,969	9,649	6,641	3,008	14,372	371,597
11		371,597	9,290	6,346	2,944	14,436	357,161
12		357,161	8,929	6,065	2,864	14,516	342,645
13		342,645	8,566	5,795	2,771	14,609	328,036
14		328,036	8,201	5,537	2,664	14,716	313,320
15		313,320	7,833	5,292	2,541	14,839	298,481
16		298,481	7,462	5,056	2,406	14,974	283,507
17		283,507	7,088	4,832	2,256	15,124	268,383
18		268,383	6,710	4,617	2,093	15,287	253,096
19		253,096	6,327	4,411	1,916	15,464	237,632
20		237,632	5,941	4,215	1,726	15,654	221,978
21		221,978	5,549	4,028	1,521	15,859	206,119
22		206,119	5,153	3,849	1,304	16,076	190,043
23		190,043	4,751	3,678	1,073	16,307	173,736
24		173,736	4,343	3,515	828	16,552	157,184
25	17,380	157,184	3,930	3,359	571	16,809	140,375
Buy at end of 25 years	140,000					140,000	375

ᵃ Annual lease payments are $34,760 before tax.

sale of the site of the old building that would be gained under the leasing option.

- The company would take depreciation on the new building on a double-declining-balance basis.
- The company's before-tax interest rate would be 5%; thus its after-tax rate would be 2 5%.

FINDINGS

The analysis is presented in the table on page 55. It showed that the $515,000 investment acquired under the ownership option would be amortized in 25 years; in other words, the sale-and-leaseback arrangement would have the same ultimate net cost as owning and borrowing. Because of its limited borrowing capacity and the immediate availability of the proceeds from the sale of the building, the company decided to enter into the sale-and-leaseback agreement.

The company also concluded from this analysis that, as a general rule, a sale-and-leaseback arrangement would be economically disadvantageous unless one or both of the following conditions obtained:

1. The nominal interest rate on which the lease payments were based was less than the company's current borrowing rate.

2. The sale of the company property to the lessor brought sufficient after-tax funds to serve as a significant offset to the loss of the timing benefit of the heavy early cash flow that accelerated depreciation would give the company if it owned the property.

CASE STUDY 7 ▌▌▌▌▌▌▌▌▌▌▌▌▌▌▌▌▌▌▌▌▌▌▌▌▌▌▌▌▌▌▌▌▌▌▌

Comparing the Profit Potential of Leasing and of Owning

An oil company

The company expresses its approach to lease evaluation as follows:

"In the evaluation of leasing, a comparison with purchase should be made whenever possible. Long-term leasing (for the economic life of the asset) is a form of financing in that it represents a source of capital which involves repayment obligations substantially equivalent to debt.

"To properly evaluate an investment proposal, it is necessary to determine the return exclusive of the method used to obtain funds. Financing costs are applicable to the entire corporation and should not be applied to individual projects. For example, a direct borrowing, even when its collateral is a specific project, should not have its interest or repayment schedules influence the evaluation of the business merits of the particular project. A stream of lease payments should be treated in the same manner as a stream of mortgage payments in evaluating lease proposals, and it is necessary to eliminate the portion of the lease payments representing financing cost from the cash stream.

"For purposes of evaluating methods of comparing purchase and lease, we have developed a 'base case' example, the figures from which are used in the opposite table. We have selected figures for the base-case example which generate operating cash income resulting in a marginal (7.5%) discounted-cash-flow return under purchase, and have used the same operating income for the leasing comparison. A purchase price of $100,000 is assumed, divided into $60,000 for buildings and $40,000 for land. A 20-year useful life is projected, with depreciation figured on the sum of the years' digits basis. The land value of $40,000 is assumed to remain constant. Under the leasing alternative, the lease payments represent the annual payment necessary to pay principal and interest on a loan of $100,000 at 6% over twenty years assuming the maximum long-term AAA borrowing rate is 5%.

"The method of evaluating lease proposals that is suggested puts leasing on a comparable basis with purchase by eliminating from the evaluation the costs of financing (the table shows an ownership alternative on the left side and a leasing alternative on the right). The lease payments have been capitalized at 5%, representing the company's presumed maximum before-tax cost of direct borrowing. The difference between the purchase price of $100,000 and the investment equivalent of $108,644 (i.e., the capitalized value of the rentals) reflects the difference of 1% between the company's 5% cost of borrowing and the lessor's assumed interest rate

Comparison of Purchase and Lease

Year	(1) (Investment) and After-Tax Operating Cash Income	(2) Tax Saving at 54% on Accelerated Depreciation (SYD Basis)	(3) Net Cash Flow (Col. 1 + 2)	(4) Present Value of Col. 3 — DCF @ 7%	(5) Present Value of Col. 3 — DCF @ 8%	(6) (Investment Equivalent) and After-Tax Operating Cash Income	(7) Total Lease Payments	(8) Interest Factor @ 5%	(9) Principal Portion (Col. 7 − 8)	(10) Tax Saving on Principal Portion (54% of Col. 9)	(11) After-Tax Oper. Savings & Tax Saving on "Principal" (Net Cash Flow) (Col. 6 + 10)	(12) Present Value of Col. 11 — DCF @ 6%	(13) Present Value of Col. 11 — DCF @ 7%
0	(100,000)	—	(100,000)	(100,000)	(100,000)	(108,644)					(108,644)	(108,644)	(108,644)
1	6,100	3,078	9,178	8,578	8,498	6,100	8,718	5,432	3,286	1,774	7,874	7,429	7,359
2	7,000	2,916	9,916	8,660	8,501	7,000	8,718	5,268	3,450	1,863	8,863	7,888	7,741
3	7,000	2,785	9,785	7,987	7,767	7,000	8,718	5,095	3,623	1,956	8,956	7,519	7,311
4	7,000	2,625	9,625	7,343	7,074	7,000	8,718	4,914	3,804	2,054	9,054	7,172	6,907
5	7,000	2,462	9,462	6,746	6,440	7,000	8,718	4,724	3,994	2,156	9,156	6,842	6,528
6	7,000	2,300	9,300	6,194	5,861	7,000	8,718	4,524	4,194	2,265	9,265	6,532	6,173
7	7,000	2,171	9,171	5,711	5,351	7,000	8,718	4,315	4,403	2,378	9,378	6,237	5,840
8	7,000	2,009	9,009	5,243	4,868	7,000	8,718	4,095	4,623	2,496	9,496	5,958	5,527
9	7,000	1,847	8,847	4,812	4,425	7,000	8,718	3,863	4,855	2,622	9,622	5,695	5,233
10	7,000	1,685	8,685	4,415	4,023	7,000	8,718	3,621	5,097	2,752	9,752	5,446	4,957
11	7,000	1,555	8,555	4,064	3,669	7,000	8,718	3,366	5,352	2,890	9,890	5,210	4,699
12	7,000	1,393	8,393	3,726	3,333	7,000	8,718	3,098	5,620	3,035	10,035	4,987	4,456
13	7,000	1,231	8,231	3,416	3,027	7,000	8,718	2,817	5,901	3,187	10,187	4,776	4,228
14	7,000	1,069	8,069	3,129	2,747	7,000	8,718	2,522	6,196	3,346	10,346	4,576	4,012
15	7,000	940	7,940	2,877	2,503	7,000	8,718	2,212	6,506	3,513	10,513	4,387	3,810
16	7,000	778	7,778	2,634	2,270	7,000	8,718	1,887	6,831	3,689	10,689	4,207	3,620
17	7,000	616	7,616	2,411	2,059	7,000	8,718	1,545	7,173	3,873	10,873	4,038	3,442
18	7,000	454	7,454	2,206	1,865	7,000	8,718	1,187	7,531	4,067	11,067	3,877	3,275
19	7,000	324	7,324	2,025	1,697	7,000	8,718	810	7,908	4,270	11,270	3,725	3,116
20	7,000	162	7,162	1,851	1,536	7,000	8,718	415	8,297	4,480	11,480	3,579	2,966
Residual value	40,000	—	40,000	10,336	8,580	—					—	—	—
Total	79,100	32,400	111,500	4,364	(3,906)	30,456	174,360	65,716	108,644	58,666	89,122	1,436	(7,444)

Purchase: Interpolating, DCF return on investment is 7.5%.

Lease: Interpolating, return on investment is 6.2%.

Notes:

Purchase

1. Investment, residual land value, and after-tax operating cash income are given in Column 1.
2. Depreciation on $60,000 is calculated on a sum of the years' digit basis, and tax savings are calculated at 54%.
3. Net cash flow is the summation of Columns 1 and 2.
4. Column 3 is shown discounted at 7% and 8% by Columns 4 and 5, respectively. By interpolation, the correct rate of return is found to be 7.5%.

Lease

1. The investment equivalent (Column 6) equals the annual lease payments described in 2 below capitalized at 5%. The after-tax operating cash income is the same as the purchase side, Col. 1. However, no residual land value is credited to lease.
2. Lease payments of $8,718 per year, (Column 7) are calculated to retire a debt of $100,000 in twenty years at 6% interest for purposes of this example.
3. The lease payments are split between interest costs at 5% and principal retirement of the $108,644 debt equivalent in the interest factor and principal portion columns. (Nos. 8 and 9)
4. Tax savings on principal portion (Column 10) are calculated at 54% and added to the after-tax operating cash income in Col. 6 to total the net cash flow in Column 11. Interest expense and tax savings on interest expense are not considered in the calculation.
5. The discounted cash flow of leasing (Column 11) is calculated using the same techniques in Columns 12 and 13 as used under the purchase alternatives in Columns 3, 4, and 5.

of 6%. We have assumed 6% to be the lessor's borrowing cost because, generally, his borrowing cost would be higher than our own rate. In this illustration, the profit of the lessor has been ignored, though in actual practice this would be an additional cost factor under leasing and thus the combined interest/profit factor would almost always exceed 6%, perhaps by a substantial margin. In the rare case where the interest rate and principal repayment are less than ours would be under direct borrowing, the lease alternative will look attractive accordingly.

"Under the purchase arrangement the depreciation charge gives rise to a stream of tax savings, normally at an accelerated rate (sum of the years' digits) which is not normally available under a lease. Assuming a direct borrowing under similar terms, which could be made to provide funds, the annual loan payment contains both interest and repayment of principal. The interest portion is deductible for tax purposes and therefore results in a tax saving, but is not credited to a rate of return analysis under ownership. There are no tax savings in connection with the principal repayments under a borrowing. However, under a lease, which is the equivalent of a direct borrowing, both interest and principal are deductible for tax purposes. Therefore, the lease should have the interest set aside as in ownership, and the tax savings arising from the amortization of principal should be added to the cash flow since this replaces tax savings on depreciation of the owned asset, to which the lease is not entitled. The amortization will also cover land, but it must be remembered that the salvage value is given up, although certain lease features can lessen this impact. The table shows that under these

assumptions ownership is the superior method of financing."

CONCLUSION

The company has drawn the following conclusions from the forgoing example:

"Since the 'investment equivalent' of the lease, which is $8,644 more than the purchase price, measures the volume of the lease debt undertaken, we, in viewing our own internal financial position, consider that if we decide to lease, we effectively borrow an amount equal to the total investment equivalent regardless of whether lenders or financial analysts judge the effective debt of the lease to be either more or less. Thus, the total funds 'borrowed' must earn a suitable return on their commitment to a specific use, i.e., a return on an investment in leased facilities. Therefore, if the facilities are to be leased, an additional $8,644 must be justified in the economics of the proposed investment. That is, an acceptable after-tax rate of return of 7.5%, applicable to the investment when owned, must be earned on this additional $8,644. Profit generated by the facilities is, of course, the same regardless of the mechanics of acquisition. Due largely to the inclusion in the lease payments of amortization of nondepreciable land, *total* tax benefits attributable to leasing are somewhat higher (although their timing is unfavorable). But the land itself is lost at the termination of the lease. That adverse impact, coupled with the need to produce a return on the additional $8,644 in the investment base, results in a rate of return on the total investment equivalent of only 6.2%."